h Series
Number 31

W9-DGP-411

Visible Solutions for Invisible Students: Helping Sophomores Succeed

Laurie A. Schreiner

Jerry Pattengale

Editors

National Resource Center for The First-Year Experience & Students In Transition
University of South Carolina, 2000

Cite as:

Schreiner, L. A. & Pattengale, J. (Eds.). (2000). *Visible solutions for invisible students: Helping sophomores succeed* (Monograph No. 31). Columbia, SC: University of South Carolina, National Resource Center for The First-Year Experience and Students In Transition.

Sample chapter citation:

Juillerat, S. (Ed.) (2000). Assessing the expectations and satisfactions of sophomores. In L. A.Schreiner & J. Pattengale. (Eds.), *Visible solutions for invisible students: Helping sophomores succeed* (Monograph No. 31) (pp. 19-29). Columbia, SC: University of South Carolina, National Resource Center for The First-Year Experience and Students In Transition.

Additional copies of this monograph may be ordered at $30 each from the National Resource Center for The First-Year Experience and Students in Transition, University of South Carolina, 1629 Pendleton Street, Columbia, SC 29208. Telephone (803) 777-6029.

Special gratitude is expressed to Jean Henscheid, Associate Director; Tracy L. Skipper, Editorial Projects Coordinator; and Katrina Chandler and Scott Slawinski, Assistant Editors, for editing this monograph; and to Doug Wood, Assistant Editor, for layout and design.

ISBN Number: 1-889271-33-0

Table Of Contents

What Is The Sophomore Slump And Why Should We Care?

by Jerry Pattengale and Laurie A. Schreiner

Our years of experience and direct observation on campuses across the nation have led us to conclude that sophomores receive the least attention of any class. While a growing number of institutions are experiencing some success in reducing first-year attrition, the question remains has this successful programming merely postponed the inevitable attrition to the sophomore year?

Believing they have succeeded with this cohort of students, institutions appear to relax their vigilance and support. Our observations suggest that continued programming and services are thought to be no longer necessary as students move successfully into their second year of college. And because sophomores are not fully into their majors or have yet to settle decisively on a major, we have noted that they receive little faculty attention.

Our experience is that sophomores benefit from a small number of special programs, few contacts with major professors, few positions of campus leadership, and little attention from student development personnel. The unintended result is that sophomores are virtually ignored from all sides of the institution, yet current research confirms that sophomores have some of the highest expectations and strongest needs of any group of students on campus (Juillerat, 1999 and in this monograph). The cost of ignoring those needs is beginning to be seen in higher-than-expected rates of sophomore attrition. Institutions may be on the road to reducing first-year attrition, but without providing ongoing programs, services, and support to sophomores, efforts seem to be only postponing the inevitable until the end of the sophomore year.

Is this "sophomore slump" real and, if so, how do we define it? As bored second-year students slouching at their desks? As GPAs taking a nosedive in the second year, when students finally have to face all those courses they avoided as first-year students? As dry spells on exams? As overall poor performance? As apathy and lack of motivation? Or is it a slump in the retention rate we would normally expect to see from the second to the third year? Actually, we believe, it is any and all of the above. The sophomore slump is not just a higher-than-expected attrition rate from the second to the third year of college. Leaving college altogether or transferring to another college are not the only symptoms of the slump. Even when sophomores remain in higher education, we have seen many suffer from reduced motivation or apathy, declining grade point averages, or a letdown from their first year.

If, as we suspect, the slump is real, what are its causes and what are its cures? Are there, in fact, unique developmental issues among sophomores contributing to predictable incidents in the second year of college—incidents that can culminate in a decision to leave college? And even for successful sophomores who remain enrolled, the question is whether educators can effectively intervene to address motivational issues so that the sophomore year is more rewarding for these students.

Our experience suggests that sophomores often begin college with high hopes—and unrealistic expectations. Baker (1985) refers to this as the "matriculant myth"—the idea that college is going to be much better than it actually is. With all the support and programming that institutions are investing in

the first year, reality often does not hit until the sophomore year, when the institution relaxes or even withdraws its support and attention. We have seen sophomores who are left on their own to navigate an intensified curriculum, to adjust their plans and dreams of becoming a physician when they get a D- in biology, to struggle through general education requirements they avoided in the first year, to find their niche on campus, and to figure out what they want to do with their lives as the clock ticks toward graduation.

We have observed that, for some sophomores, the negative behavior patterns or academic struggles that began in their first year and were tolerated by the institution because they were first-year students are now beginning to catch up with them—at the same time that the institution tightens its standards and increases its expectations. Thus the sophomore year becomes almost a "weeding out" process by the institution, both in and out of the classroom.

On the other hand, perhaps this weeding out process is a healthy and natural part of ensuring quality graduates from our institutions. Perhaps a letdown from the first year is a natural and inevitable part of the student maturation process. However, the fact remains, if student success is the main objective of educational institutions, educators must be concerned about the experiences of all of their students, including sophomores. If the goal is to facilitate the learning process to equip students for a lifetime of learning, educators should be alarmed if sophomores are falling into a curricular and programmatic gap—often with memories of special first-year initiatives and knowledge of major classes enjoyed by their junior and senior colleagues.

If sophomores are not successful, institutions are not successful. And the costs are high for both institutions and students. After investing two years and 60 academic credits by the end of the sophomore year, the decision to leave costs the student considerably more than a similar decision made after a bumpy first or second semester. By intentionally focusing on sophomores and their needs, expectations, and experiences, educators can begin to prevent symptoms of the slump so that more sophomores return as successful juniors energized by the learning process, confident of their plans and goals, and eagerly anticipating continued involvement with the institution.

But are sophomore attrition and reduced motivation problems serious enough to receive significant attention and funding priorities on our campuses? Before we began writing about sophomore issues, we needed to make sure our assumptions were indeed valid, that empirical studies matched the anecdotal and sporadic calls for help that we had heard from this population. Based on what we have found, we believe that the slump warrants considerable attention for inherently good and fiscally responsible reasons. Besides the obvious attrition problem among sophomores (reason enough to dub it the "slump"), the authors in this monograph report some personal developmental needs for sophomores that are perhaps the biggest "surprise" for student success teams.

The first section of this monograph lays the philosophical and experiential groundwork for our exploration of the sophomore year. The first chapter, written by Michael Boivin and associates, identifies the often unique challenges of the sophomore year and defines the sophomore slump as a developmental issue. In the second chapter, Stephanie Juillerat reports on the expectation and satisfaction levels of thousands of sophomore students from public and private four-year institutions. In Chapter 3, Jerry Pattengale summarizes the perceptions of higher education professionals who were asked their impressions of the needs of sophomores at their institutions.

In the second section of the monograph, we attempt to address the needs of sophomores and explore programmatic and institutional

responses to those needs. Jerry Gaff examines curricular issues contributing to sophomore success in Chapter 4, while Edward "Chip" Anderson and Laurie Schreiner assert that academic advising holds particular promise as a major vehicle for preventing sophomore attrition and increasing student motivation and success. In Chapter 6, Philip D. Gardner highlights the disconnect between sophomores and the academy, and offers suggestions for creating linkages, especially in the area of career services. All these mechanisms working in concert, we propose, have great potential for helping sophomores. In Chapter 7, Scott Evenbeck and associates explore the institutional response to this unique population, revealing the programs and services needed by, but not always offered to, second-year students. In the final chapter, we are joined by John N. Gardner as we summarize our findings and make recommendations for meeting the needs of sophomore students. The appendices include data from Juillerat's survey (reported on in Chapter 2) and an annotated bibliography on the sophomore slump compiled by Stephanie M. Foote.

The focus of our efforts has often been on at-risk first-year students, yet there are still many at-risk students among the sophomore population. Just as in the first year, there are obstacles to student success that are landmines scattered throughout the sophomore landscape. Many universities are realizing that re-entry problems are common among their sophomores. Some schools, like Stanford University, even hold special summer camps (or colleges) to assist groups of sophomores to adjust to the second year. Other universities assign special sophomore advisors. The College of William and Mary has established a Sophomore Board and a sophomore newsletter to address the specific needs of second-year students. In the Allegheny Mountains in early September, the sophomores of Cedar Crest College are on retreat—dubbed "The Sophomore Quest" by the student success staff. In San Marcos, Texas, sophomores this past fall were serving as peer leaders in the first-year seminar course of Southwest Texas State University. These programs appear to be making a difference in the attitudes and success levels of sophomores across the country and are described in greater detail in Chapter 3.

Much of the research on the sophomore slump, like Joyce Wilder's "The Sophomore Slump: A Complex Developmental Period that Contributes to Attrition" (1993), identifies some important findings from small groups of students on a limited number of campuses. This monograph also includes research conducted with thousands of students at both public and private colleges across the country. Both approaches are important and are synthesized here to help provide answers to a number of complex issues.

By pulling together a variety of views on sophomores and examining sophomores' unique needs and issues, we hope to provide institutions not only with a blueprint for addressing sophomore attrition, but also for energizing sophomores so they may benefit more from their educations. Our hope is to enable more students from more institutions to move from the sophomore slump to sophomore success.

References

Baker, R.W., McNeil, O.V., & Siryk, B. (1985). Expectation and reality in freshman adjustment to college. *Journal of Counseling Psychology, 32*(1), 94-103.

Juillerat, S. (1999, January). *Using student satisfaction data to impact institutional effectiveness.* Paper presented at the annual conference of the Quality/Retention Project of the Council for Christian Colleges & Universities, Tampa, FL.

Wilder, J. (1993, Spring). The sophomore slump: A complex developmental period that contributions to attrition. *College Student Affairs Journal, 12,* 18-27.

Meeting the Challenges of the Sophomore Year

by Michael Boivin, Gwen A. Fountain and Bayard (By) Baylis

Chapter 1

While doing telephone interviews at one school with former students who had left during their first two years, Boivin, Beuthin, and Hauger (1993) noted that the reasons students gave for leaving during their second year were different from those pertaining to first-year attrition. Students leaving during or after their first year typically talked about issues related to their own academic, social, financial, or motivational struggles and challenges.

Students leaving in the second year more often cited issues or problems pertaining to the school itself and its ability to deliver in terms of the students' initial expectations. Conducting a similar interview with students in that same cohort who had stayed at the college, we found the same to be true. Although these were peers who were still enrolled, many had considered leaving the school at some point, but the issues were different for those who had seriously considered leaving early on as opposed to those who had more recently considered leaving as they completed their sophomore year.

It may be argued that both groups, in their struggle for success and belonging in college were challenged by the "sophomore slump." However, we are not sure the term adequately describes the true nature of this phenomenon. In comparison to the transition faced in the first year, some student development theorists might conclude that students can work through this sophomore inertia with a little inspiration, re-energizing, or a bit of a push on the part of professors and college staff. However, our belief is that the challenges threatening student success in the second year are, in some ways, distinct from those of the first year and are just as significant.

1

Furthermore, the challenges inherent in the sophomore year are important to understand, because in some ways they strike at the very heart of the mission and purpose of American higher education. Unless consideration is given to the sophomore year experience, successive cohorts of first-year students will continue to weather the storms of first-year transition, only to bail out of higher education when they face the serious developmental challenges which continue and even intensify in the sophomore year.

In their developmental perspective of the sophomore slump, Lemons and Richmond (1987) conclude that of the seven major "vectors" or areas of college student development described in Chickering's classic study (1969), four are particularly salient. For the sophomore, these are achieving competence, developing autonomy, establishing identity, and developing purpose. Marcus (1973) suggests that higher education fails to consistently help students achieve these goals and that a renewed emphasis is necessary within American colleges and universities to intentionally socialize students into the subculture of higher education and attend to these developmental realities. The strategies of transformational education described in the second half of this chapter are one way to meet this challenge.

After describing the distinct challenges faced by students in the second year as compared to the first year of college, we will elaborate on the four Chickering vectors emphasized by Lemons and Richmond (1987). We will then provide examples of existing programs that attempt to address those developmental vectors of concern in the sophomore year. Finally, we conclude with an advocacy of comprehensive interventions for sophomores that are holistic and founded on mentoring relationships within an environment focused on transformational education.

What Is So Different About Year Two?

Considering the time, energy, and resources that many colleges and universities now invest in the transitional issues faced by students in their first college year, the call for concern over the "sophomore slump" might seem a bit overdone. How could the second-year concerns be as serious as the challenges posed in the first year?

The traditional first-year student comes to college typically facing self-management issues posed by independent living circumstances in the residence hall and campus community. In addition, the first-year student typically encounters a higher level of academic responsibility, as well as a distancing or even loss of the family, peer, and community support, intensifying the individuation process for that student. Finally, the first-year student must acclimate to and succeed within a campus culture that he or she may be ill equipped to understand, much less thrive within (Banning, 1989). Small wonder that over 70% of American colleges and universities now have a first-year student experience program of some sort to help students persevere through such challenges on their campuses and persist into their second year (Barefoot & Fidler, 1996).

First-year students, their families, society, and the academy expect this transition to college to require work and commitment from everyone involved. However, by the sophomore year, it is usually expected that sophomores will have adapted so that we may turn our attention to the next wave of first-year students.

Sophomores are "between" in every respect. They are no longer naïve in their thinking about what college is, so they may become cynical and disillusioned. They often have not committed to a specific major, yet they may be painfully aware of what they are not interested in or good at doing. Sometimes that failed interest is something they previously had indicated as their life's goal to friends and family. How many self-proclaimed premedical students, accountants, dancers, vocalists, computer scientists, novelists, or artists find themselves in this situation? They may begin to realize that this is their life and they must ferret out what they want for themselves and not what their parents or peers feel is best for them.

Compounding the challenges posed by this heightened burden of responsibility for sophomores in terms of life and career decisions is the greater awareness they may now have regarding what higher education can and cannot do for them. After students have weathered the storms of personal inadequacy and incompetence in that first year, they have the capacity to assume a clearer vantage point with the confidence that they really can cope with and survive the challenges of higher education. And from that vantage point, students can begin finally to take a good honest look at the institution and see clearly what the heart of it is really all about. The student may now stand judge as to whether the institution is able to deliver on its promises.

Vectors for Navigating the Sophomore Year

Achieving Competence

The above profile of the challenges faced by students in the sophomore year is supported by the work of Lemons and Richmond (1987). Sophomore students must establish a new standard of competence in the intellectual, manual skill, and interpersonal realms that exceed those adequate for high school and even the first year of college. Difficulty in the gateway or entry-level courses for the major, difficulties on the athletic field or in performance arena (e.g., art and music), difficulty in interpersonal relationships (e.g.,

dating, roommates, peer acceptance)—all of these can precipitate a crisis of confidence that may come to a head in the sophomore year.

Developing Autonomy

The first vector, establishing a new standard of competence, is closely related to the second vector, developing autonomy. In terms of the emotional independence component of autonomy, the sophomore is no longer expected to be as reliant on parental support and approval. Yet, the sophomore is perhaps most in need of that support as he or she faces a crisis of confidence in terms of changing standards of competence. Furthermore, the sophomore may still be dependent on parental support financially and is, therefore, not functionally independent. Finally, the sophomore may not yet have achieved an adequate sense of interdependence and support within the campus community to supplant the loss of parental and former peer-group dependence.

Loevinger (1976) notes that most young adults are moving from the conscientious stage of believing and accepting the rules and feeling guilty when they break them to the autonomous stage, where they develop an awareness of a range of choices and a tolerance for those who choose differently. The tasks related to this autonomous stage of development are often neglected in students' educational experiences. Willard (1999) notes that many colleges and universities limit their scope of responsibility and program interventions strictly to the academic arena and downplay the social, moral, and interpersonal needs of students. Curricular and co-curricular programming that can help students become more aware of the world of choices open to them assists students as they develop autonomy. Programs that introduce students to others who are different from themselves help students develop tolerance for differences and also assist in the development of autonomy.

Establishing Identity

How successful the sophomore is in establishing a new sense of competency and achieving a healthy interdependence within the campus community significantly determines progress in the third vector, that of establishing an identity. Achieving competence and autonomy and interdependence ultimately impacts on identity formation, self-esteem, and self-concept for these young adults.

Significant work within the field of developmental psychology focuses on identity development in a way which can be helpful in attempting to understand these issues as they relate to sophomores. In Erikson's (1968) concept of identity formation, young adults attempt to answer the question, "Who am I?" Young adulthood is marked by an "identity crisis" as the individual struggles with this question. The individual forms an identity by trying on various roles, before subsequently committing himself or herself to a particular role.

Parks (1986) contends that the college years provide the best opportunity to reshape one's identity because the college experience allows for:

1. Experimentation with varied roles
2. Exposure to credible, alternative goals and beliefs exhibited in teachers and peers
3. Experience of choice and having to make decisions for oneself
4. Meaningful achievement
5. Freedom from excessive anxiety
6. Time for reflection and introspection

She contends that as a result of their college experiences college students may enter and leave college with essentially the same expressed set of values, but with different identities from when they were first-year students.

Marcia (1987) identifies four identity statuses based upon Erikson's theory (see Figure 1). Each status represents a particular style of coping with the task of trying to define oneself. Marcia uses Erikson's concepts of crisis and commitment to define the statuses; the term "crisis" refers to one's critical exploration of occupational, religious, social, and political goals and beliefs. For Erikson and Marcia, the idea of a crisis is not necessarily negative. Crisis is an active engagement with and exploration of alternatives or competing roles and ideologies. Commitment refers to the selection of goals and beliefs from among alternatives. Because commitment carries with it a degree of permanence, once made it is not easily reversed.

For college students the areas of meaningful exploration usually include major and career choices, religious beliefs and values, political opinions, sexual standards, gender roles, and relationships. Students typically enter college in a diffused or foreclosed state. And while the college experience ought to assist students in establishing a sense of identity, Pascarella and Terenzini (1991) claim that from 40% to 67% of students graduate from college with their identity status relatively unexamined and therefore unchanged.

Perry's (1970, 1981) schema views young adulthood as a time when foundational truths are challenged and doubted, so that a period of relativism characterizes much of the college years. Students then emerge through this period of relativism into a stage that Perry termed "evolving commitment" where they can once again cautiously begin to hold to some foundational truths within a paradigm or framework for understanding life and the meaning it provides for their vocational choices and goals. But for most sophomores, Perry suggests that thinking is still dualistic, with things seen in stark relief. Transition issues are approached dualistically as well and may be viewed as a move from the "known" to the "unknown." This sense of transition, of being afloat between the known truths and the unknown future, contributes to the anxiety often felt in the sophomore year, when less support to navigate the transitions and uncertainties is available.

Developing Purpose

Achieving competence, developing autonomy, and establishing identity culminate in Chickering's fourth vector germane to the sophomore year—that of developing purpose. Developing purpose is a search for direction and commitment. As such, it encompasses not only the choice of a vocation, but also life goals, lifestyle choices, and recreational interests (Lemons & Richmond, 1987). But as Chickering (1969) notes, "Many young adults are all dressed up and don't know where to go; they have energy but no destination" (p. 15). In the tradition of film character Jim Stark, they are "rebels without a cause," or in many cases, without a clue.

As a result, many students entering the sophomore year experience a crisis of meaning and purpose. Wilder (1993) compared "decliners" (students who exhibited a 20% decline in grade point average (GPA) during sophomore year from the first year) and "maintainers" (students who maintained or improved upon their first-year GPA). He found that the most significant distinguishing traits in decliners were lack of commitment to school, absenteeism, lack of educational goals, lack of extracurricular activities, and poor perceptions of faculty-staff caring interactions.

The first author of this chapter and his colleagues have seen the same dynamic

Figure 1
Marcia's Identity Statuses Related to Crisis and Commitment

	No commitment	**Commitment**
No Crisis	*Diffused*–characterized by disinterest and detachment. In this state, a young adult has not critically explored goals and beliefs, and does not have commitments. When asked, "Why?" a diffused individual typically will respond, "Uh, I don't know. It's just something to do."	*Foreclosed*–characterized by "borrowed" commitments. In this state, the young adult has firm commitments that are not based upon any process of critical examination or exploration. When asked, "Why?" a typical response is "I've always believed that way. My parents have always believed that. That's the way it is."
Crisis	*Moratorium*–characterized by the critical examination of potential alternatives. This individual has not yet made commitments, but is actively engaged in a search for commitments. When asked, "Why?" a typical response might be, "I don't know yet, but here is what I've been thinking…"	*Achieved*–characterized by an identity achieved through the exploration and commitments based upon those critical examinations. When asked, "Why?" the achieved adolescent may reply, "Having looked at several alternatives, I think the best position on this question is because …"

consistently emerge in more than 60 phone interviews conducted over a two-year period with students leaving during or after their sophomore year from a small liberal arts college in Michigan. Many of these students, coming from a wide variety of programs, felt that they came searching for purpose and security and found neither. Within a campus culture promising community and identity, fully a third of these non-returning sophomores found no community and experienced only competitive exclusion and isolation. Almost two-thirds of these former students reported only piecemeal content and a series of disconnected hurdles in the form of general education requirements.

As Anderson and Schreiner note in their chapter on advising strategies for sophomores elsewhere in this monograph, the "myths" of a college education did not match the reality for many students. Juillerat, also in this monograph, confirms that sophomores across the nation have higher expectations for many of the services colleges provide than do students at other levels. As she notes, it would seem prudent that colleges address the mismatch between students' expectations and the reality of college life in the sophomore year beginning with helping students discover a sense of purpose for their education and their lives.

Practical Interventions to Enhance the Four Vectors for Navigating the Sophomore Year

How can colleges and universities help students find realistic meaning and purpose in their education? What can we do to assist them in moving purposefully, positively, and creatively through this time of transition? Several possibilities, categorized by Chickering's four vectors, are offered in the examples below.

Achieving Competence

At Butler University (IN) the Joining Together Project was initially designed to encourage campus organizations to plan activities in the spring that would occur during those critical first eight weeks of the first-year experience. Because the rising seniors were generally engaged in the transition to leadership positions in organizations, the leadership of this new program often fell to current sophomores and first-year students. This phenomenon brought these students into leadership positions earlier than ever before. Creating earlier opportunities to take responsibility for others and events seems to assist sophomores in finding their own way, helping them establish a sense of competence.

A second example of a program intended to engage sophomores in positions of leadership in order to enhance their identification with the university mission and their sense of competence, service, and responsibility is the Step Ahead Leadership Training (SALT) program at Indiana Wesleyan University (IWU). First-year students who feel they could benefit from additional leadership training are encouraged to apply to become part of SALT, where they attend a series of training sessions on such topics as conflict resolution, group dynamics and organization, and styles of leadership. Recently, participants in SALT were recruited to serve as peer leaders in the required first-year course at IWU, where they assisted course faculty in organizing periodic small-group meetings and the community-service activities required of all first-year students. These SALT peer leaders provided referrals for support services (counseling, academic tutoring, financial aid, and advising) to the course faculty members as they became aware of specific needs among the first-year students.

Following the first semester of this new program, the response from SALT peer leaders was positive. Consistently, the students said they felt more invested in the campus mission and felt as if they had an opportunity to contribute to incoming students in a service capacity. They said the direct faculty mentoring of these peer leaders, as well as their role as servant-leaders for first-year students, has enriched their own development.

Developing Autonomy

Another program at Butler University encourages students to establish autonomy but does so in a much more supportive and less abrupt manner than tends to be the case when the first-year program comes to an end and students are "turned loose to fend for themselves." The Leisure Links Program provides faculty up to $200 to plan outings or gatherings with small groups of first-year students and sophomores. The only requirement to receive the funds is that faculty supply the Academic Affairs Office with the names and class year of participating students, a sentence or two about the nature of the event, and receipts of expenditures for reimbursement. Surprisingly, almost as many sophomores as first-year students participated in the sponsored activities. The sophomores seemed to appreciate this opportunity to interact informally with faculty as much or more than the first-year students did. Many of the sophomores indicated real pleasure in being able to visit with faculty in an informal setting. Some also noted that they felt more confident in asking questions about issues important to them personally.

Spring Arbor College (MI) addresses the task of developing autonomy by focusing on experiences in the sophomore year that can help students become more aware of choices open to them and to develop a tolerance for differences. The Spring Arbor program is discussed in greater detail later in this chapter.

Establishing Identity

The Program Advisors Project at Butler University was originally designed to link first-year students to activities on campus, but an additional impact on sophomores has been realized. Program advisors were assigned to each living unit with responsibility for discovering what each first-year student on the unit was interested in and then letting the students know when events were occurring on campus related to their interests; finally, the program advisors were to follow up and see how many of their first-year students attended the events. Since residence hall assistants were primarily juniors and seniors, the program advisors were primarily sophomores. A program evaluation indicated that sophomores who participated as program advisors went to more on-campus events and felt more connected to campus life than those who were not program advisors. Many also seemed to feel responsible for their first-year students attending events and being involved in campus activities. This sense of responsibility seemed to help the sophomores stay more focused academically, as well.

Developing Purpose

Butler University has also created two programs that assist sophomores in developing purpose within the context of choosing a major and a career. Over the past three years, as part of the process of developing retention programs, Butler analyzed subsets of the student population that seemed to be more prone to leave the university. One group that seemed most at-risk was students enrolled in the health sciences (e.g., premedical, pre-dental, pre-physicians' assistants, and pre-pharmacy majors). The pilot project developed as a result included the creation of three faculty liaison positions, with faculty teaching first- or second-year courses in biology, chemistry, and pharmacy recruited for these positions. Their charge was to provide a neutral point for reflective listening and to offer support to students wanting to transition to other majors at Butler or at other universities. They were then able to discuss alternative career options and goals within the health care fields, to follow up with "failure to pre-register" students in the pre-health areas, and to coordinate with the Pre-professional Studies Office in meeting the needs of these students. These faculty agreed to post and keep extended office hours and to advertise their role as "transition faculty" who desired to discuss life alternatives with students. They agreed to take time to learn about alternative health care career options and to meet with the head of pre-professional studies and the Dean of Academic Affairs on a regular basis. It was understood that these special faculty liaison advisors would only be an alternative to students' regular advisors during the short transition period where students needed to explore other options with a more neutral faculty member.

Results of the spring 1999 pilot indicated that 50% fewer pre-health students left the university than during the previous year. The faculty who participated said they had assisted at least three students in making a different choice of major. One faculty liaison interacted with more than 30 students during the six weeks of the pilot. The faculty liaisons recommended the program be continued for the coming year.

The second program designed to assist primarily sophomores in developing a purpose was piloted one day a week in the spring semester of 1999. A counseling intern was assigned as an "academic transitions counselor." This person was available in her office in the Academic Affairs area one day a week to meet any student advising needs on a "walk in" basis. This academic transitions counselor also focused on retention by coordinating and working with an Academic Peer Counseling Group, working with students who failed to pre-register for classes during the spring pre-registration period, and making contact with all students who requested transcripts with an intention to leave the University.

The counselor met with at least two students a day and contacted many others by telephone and e-mail. Follow-up evaluations indicated that these contacts resulted in several students remaining at the University. The majority of the students contacted and counseled were year-end first-year students or rising sophomores. Many indicated they appreciated a neutral party, unrelated to their declared

major, to talk to and to assist them in gathering the information they needed to work through difficult life decisions. The program was slated to continue on a full-time basis in the fall of 1999.

A second example of a program which helps sophomores develop a sense of purpose is the mentoring program at the University of Michigan entitled the Undergraduate Research Opportunity Program (UROP). This program matches first- and second-year students for year-long research apprenticeship programs with an upper-level peer advisor and top research faculty in a variety of disciplines at the university, based on the students' areas of intellectual interest. The program provides a stipend to the student to work with that faculty sponsor in a senior/junior scholar collaboration with the expectation that they will pursue and publish their work together. Students present their work in the form of a research poster at a final awards session and banquet recognizing both student and faculty members. The program has grown significantly from its inception in the number of student participants and faculty and has now been recognized by the university as one of its "Programs of Excellence."

Transformational Education: Strategies for Addressing Sophomore Challenges

The common thread among all of the above interventions is that they go beyond an exclusive focus on teaching students disciplinary content in the sophomore year. They are designed to move these students intentionally into the realm of establishing a mentoring relationship with a faculty (or non-faculty professional) person who can bring students alongside him or her and model for them the pursuit of a profession. As the sophomore student begins to see his/her mentor model the pursuit of a discipline with virtue and integrity, that student is more likely to begin to see substance in what the baccalaureate experience has to offer. If that program has the additional benefit of providing sophomores with the opportunity to mentor or invest in other students (such as first-year students), they may well find fulfilling and meaningful educational enrichment in such service. This "transformational education" is the creation of a learning environment in which the student's whole person is shaped as he or she interacts with faculty and other students in a process of making meaning of the college experience. Such education is characterized by four major features: (a) character development, or education of the whole person, (b) "scaffolding," or providing an appropriate balance of challenge and support to students, (c) praxis, or being changed by doing, and (d) mentoring, or even "discipleship" or apprenticeship within the student's discipline. Because these features are particularly powerful in ameliorating the effects of the sophomore slump, they are discussed at length below.

Character Development

Sir John Templeton (1999), founder of the Templeton Foundation and the Templeton Honor Roll for Character Development, believes that parents, students, educators, and businesses are realizing anew the importance of character development as part of a student's education. He suggests they are re-emphasizing the notion that education can (and should) play an important role in the development of conscience, character, citizenship, and social responsibility. Students gaining a sense of growth in these areas as a means of undergirding their professional preparation will believe they are better prepared to make a contribution in their chosen professional fields as leaders. Particularly in the sophomore year, as students experience greater pressure to decide on a major and a career, attention to the role of character development and educating the "whole person" becomes an important task.

Scaffolding

Richard Butman, Professor of Psychology at Wheaton College (IL), uses the metaphor of "scaffolding" in the critical years of university life to communicate the key components of a transformational educational model (Butman, 1999). Scaffolding for the sophomore can be characterized as the proper blend of challenge and support as students emerge from the transitions of the first year and begin in earnest to seek the natural learning community of their disciplinary choice in their second year. The student has the support for a personal journey encompassing intellectual, moral, faith, ego, and identity development. But by characterizing this balance of challenge and support as "scaffolding," there is the recognition that this framework is a temporary structure which can—and should—be set aside later by the student.

As Van Wicklin, Burwell, and Butman (1994) note:

> One theme that runs through the research-based work of both Chickering and Astin is the need for a community of faculty and peers that offers a balance of challenge and support integral to the objectives of liberal education. Too much challenge without support may make it difficult to sustain learning in the face of powerful dissonance, while at the same time make it tempting to discount, defend or retreat. Too much support or homogeneity with little challenge may not nudge one out of apathy or complacency. (p. 92)

In speaking to the same point, Parks (1986) claims that faculty members have the responsibility to be "centers of conflict" (p. 145). But in challenging students to move beyond a set worldview, professors should not relinquish support too early. The faculty must be there to assist the student in working through the rebuilding of his or her beliefs. Parks says,

. . . if the moment of conflict is to be sustained so as to make possible a new composing of truth and faith, the conflict must be held in a "context of rapport" which is to say, held in community, in trust. Teachers must have staying power. The conflict is creative only if one is not left alone with it, or otherwise has to defend it. We can face the largest challenges before us only together. (p. 145)

The role of a teacher then becomes critical in providing this appropriate balance of challenge and support. Butman (1993) feels the qualities of effective teachers in the collegiate setting include competence in and enthusiasm for the discipline, along with an insatiable thirst for knowledge. These traits are then coupled with the ability to make the course content relevant through ample illustrations and helpful examples and the ability to motivate students to take active responsibility for the learning process by providing good structure and support. These features are made complete by a teacher's willingness to be a credible role model who inspires hope and confidence. As he notes,

I am deeply convinced that the effective teacher is not a pleader, not a performer, not a huckster, 'but a confident, exuberant guide on expeditions of shared responsibility'— perhaps most like a mountaineering guide. . . . We must never lose sight of the magic and majesty of the learning experience, nor should we forget that good teaching is a self-eradicating process. Rather, it must be a highly active and interactive task of shared responsibilities and risks. (Butman, 1993, p. 255)

In this characterization of the effective teacher, Butman captures the critical ingredient of effective mentoring and discipleship within a natural learning community. Such a college environment would foster what Butman terms "engaged students" and would be characterized by good peer interactions; good student-faculty interactions as students have ready access to role models and mentors; a desire to create an active, collaborative learning environment; an

intentionality about choices that allows a student to move beyond his/her intellectual, emotional, and cultural comfort zones; and active commitment seeking by students exploring alternatives (Butman, 1999).

Praxis

Ultimately, the notion of praxis is at the heart of transformational education. Praxis is a concept derived from sociology suggesting that we are changed by doing (Campolo, 1984). That is, as we engage in behaviors that lead to life experiences, those experiences shape our feelings and attitudes about our world and ourselves. As these feelings and attitudes take form, we begin to fashion the accounts or stories that we use to explain to ourselves and to others why we do what we do and who we are. These are what we term "beliefs" or "understanding." In short, our beliefs come about as we make sense of our experiences and behaviors in contrast to the traditional educational model where we must first change beliefs through knowledge in order to change behavior and experience.

Colleges and universities have increasingly recognized the importance of learning by doing and have incorporated various forms of internships or service-learning requirements, typically at the departmental level. Kalamazoo College (MI), for example, requires all of its sophomores to engage in some practical "career service" experience within the major during the sophomore year. These sophomores may not end up choosing that area as their final academic major or career option, but they are likely to have an experience in a practical setting apart from their classroom education that engages them and challenges them to seek relevant connections and applications from the theory and content.

Butler University has several sophomore-level service-learning courses. That is, they have required components that relate classroom activities to community activity—

either in the form of community-based research or in the form of volunteer service. The key distinction of these "real-world" learning experiences is that they encourage students to use the experiences reflectively to analyze long-term solutions and structural strategies in solving systemic problems within the communities and organizations in which they are working. In other words, they are encouraged to "think connectively" as they evaluate their experiences. Such experiences are especially important for the sophomore. Reflective and discipline-relevant volunteerism challenges the sophomore cognitively, vocationally, ethically, and socially as that student attempts to assimilate these experiences into his or her educational goals and mission.

Mentoring and Discipleship

The most powerful type of experience within the praxis of human development is the human relationship. That is why mentoring and discipleship within a context of service learning, volunteerism, or engagement in an on-campus learning community are so vital if we are to effectively address the challenges of the sophomore year. As the first-year student emerges from the transitional challenges of the first year, the most urgent need is not disciplinary knowledge or information, even though that is often what an academic program offers. It is, instead, relationship and community, through which one can engage in the practices and virtues of the discipline, and through which one will ultimately derive the beliefs and understanding that will guide his or her pursuit of the profession with wisdom. Knowledge of the discipline is incidental to this process, not fundamental to it. First-year students may believe us when we try to tell them the answers that first year, because they are still unsure about themselves and trust the academic authorities upon which they must depend for their initial survival. But sophomores, by and large, have learned the game; they may question or at least be uncertain about our authority, and they may

not care about our answers until they experience the questions for themselves alongside of us in a mentoring relationship. Transformational educators would suggest that mentoring relationships are important at this juncture.

The qualities of this mentoring relationship, as posited by Chickering (1969) are particularly germane to the sophomore experience. The first quality of this relationship is accessibility, referring to both in-class and out-of-class availability. Faculty members should recognize the presence of students in their classes and be open to student questions, be willing to spend time with students, engage in conversations with students, keep regular office hours, and be a visible presence on campus.

Secondly, a mentor must be genuine with students, willing to disclose him- or herself in an appropriate way that contributes to students' growth. Mentors share their struggles as a way of guiding students through similar situations, and they treat each student as a unique individual.

And finally, faculty should understand their students' and their diverse needs. A mentor can best help students when he or she knows the individual student's strengths and weaknesses, life goals, family situation, dreams, hopes, and values. As Astin (1993) noted after reviewing more than 20 years of CIRP data, faculty are second only to peers in impacting students' perceptions of their college experience. And the most important aspects of faculty involvement included positive attitudes toward general education and more time spent in teaching and advising compared to research and writing.

To be a mentor, there must also be a "mentee," who is also engaged in the process. The most successful students have come to appreciate active approaches to learning, are learning to be extrinsically motivated, have built relationships with other academically minded students, and have sought out faculty whom they can trust. By virtue of their progression to the sophomore year, these students are primed for further development. It is at this point that responsive, caring mentors can have a powerful impact. For anecdotal evidence of the potential impact of mentoring on sophomore students, see the first author's account of his personal experience with mentoring in college (Boivin, 1988).

The faculty mentor plays an important role in this process of identity development of the second-year student. As Steve Garber (1996) notes in his book, *The Fabric of Faithfulness*, one characteristic of a transformational learning environment is that students are encouraged not only to develop a worldview that can make sense of life, but also to "pursue a relationship with a teacher whose life incarnates that worldview the student is learning to embrace" (p. 171).

But just as mentoring goes beyond teaching and modeling, the notion of "discipleship" goes still further. It involves more than establishing a personal relationship with students so as to guide them in the pursuit of the discipline on a more individual basis. Discipleship includes personal guidance and modeling with the expressed aim of encouraging the disciple not only within the discipline or profession, but also within a particular worldview and value commitment that provide a foundation for pursuing the profession with excellence.

To illustrate, Indiana Wesleyan University has recently initiated several pilot programs designed to foster a "discipleship within the discipline." In one such program, sophomore-level nursing students are assigned to spend the day with a recent nursing graduate "on the job" to experience a typical workday beside that professional and to see first hand how that graduate pursues the profession. Both the nursing and religion departments hold special convocation events in the fall that welcome

students into the major. A number of other majors hold similar special events for inductees into their disciplinary honor societies. These initiatives foster a sense of mentoring and serve as a rite of passage into a natural learning community that formally recognizes the sophomore as a new and important member of the profession. A benefit of membership in this community is the opportunity both to be mentored and to mentor others.

To summarize, mentoring relationships within the discipline shape lives and provide meaning to the sophomore. They do so by orchestrating experiences in an intentional manner (praxis) through the most powerful vehicles available, human relationships and community. Discipleship goes far in shaping lives by incorporating the power of mentoring (and hence praxis) within the context of virtue, character development, and a coherent worldview. In doing so, not only are transformational experiences at work in human mentoring relationships, but students' beliefs and understanding of who they are and where they fit in the world are also stirred and challenged in meaningful ways. This is the definition of transformational education, an approach, we contend, that offers the greatest possibility of thwarting the sophomore slump.

Illustrations of Transformational Education

Important lessons about transformational education, as it relates to the sophomore year, can be gleaned from the research generated by a project co-directed by By Baylis, Academic Vice President at Indiana Wesleyan University, and Karen Longman, Vice President of Academic Affairs at Greenville College (IL). This collaborative research project involved approximately 50 member schools of the Council for Christian Colleges and Universities (CCCU), a cooperative organization of colleges and universities rooted in the liberal arts and committed to the integration of faith, scholarship, and service. This project, entitled *Taking Values Seriously:*

Assessing the Mission of Church-Related Higher Education, examined students as they entered college, as they graduated, and two years after they were out of college, to determine what effect the college experience had on students enrolled at these institutions (Baylis, Burwell, & Dewey, 1994; Baylis, 1995; Baylis, 1996; Baylis, 1997a; Baylis, 1997b).

The project examined both students and faculty to determine what values they brought to the classroom. The project included both quantitative and qualitative assessment methods, using pencil and paper surveys and videotaped interviews. Both longitudinal and cross-sectional designs were used, along with standardized, nationally normed instruments from the Higher Education Research Institute (HERI) and instruments constructed specifically for this project. Approximately 19,500 entering first-year students, 11,500 graduating seniors, 2,500 alumni, and 2,200 faculty provided data.

The results of these standardized surveys indicate that the values expressed by students as they entered their first year of college did not change perceptibly as they graduated and became alumni. The question then becomes, what difference did the college education make? Feldman and Newcomb (1969) offer the relevant social accentuation phenomenon, which suggests that students are attracted to colleges which support their values and belief systems, gravitate toward other students with similar values, and thus remain enrolled only if the college environment supports and rewards those values.

The degree to which students become open to change seems to offer one clue. Students typically enter college in a diffused or foreclosed state (i.e. borrowed commitments and the absence of critical exploration of positions), which was found to be the case among students participating in this study, where 65% to 85% of the first-year students expressing a foreclosed identity. As noted earlier, Pascarella and Terenzini (1991) found

that from 40% to 67% of students enter and graduate from college with their identity status relatively unexamined and therefore unchanged. In this study, 40% of the college seniors were still identity foreclosed, a change from the original 65 to 85% who were foreclosed as first-year students (VanWicklin, Burwell & Butman, 1994).

What about the campuses studied encourages students to move from a foreclosed to an achieved identity at this greater rate? The member institutions of the CCCU believe that four years of a Christian, liberal arts education should bring students to a point of critical commitment, or at least to the point of engaging in a personal examination of one's goals and beliefs.

The institutions in this study have committed themselves and their resources to help the entering students advance their level of identity development. Based on this research, four aspects of their learning environments seem to foster identity development: (a) the sense of community on campus, (b) a collaborative academic ethos that provides a balance of challenge and support, (c) strong student-faculty interactions, and (d) the encouragement and opportunity to engage in service learning or cross-cultural experiences.

According to Chickering (1969), identity formation is greatly assisted when students can live in close interaction with persons of diverse backgrounds where close friendships can be forged and meaningful, spontaneous discussions occur. The institutions participating in this study reported significantly higher student satisfaction with the sense of community than did students at other four-year private colleges (Schreiner, 2000).

Identity development also can be fostered when students experience feedback regarding personal strengths and weaknesses. Students develop identity better when the educational experience does not pressure them into a highly competitive environment where academic achievement predominates. A classroom reward system based on cooperative completion of assignments is more influential on students' identity development than one based on competitive striving for grades (Chickering, 1969). This is not to downplay academic standards, but to suggest an examination of the atmosphere surrounding those standards.

Recently published results of interviews on the Dordt College (Sioux Center, Iowa) campus (Bussema, 1999) investigate not only identity development, but also the stage of faith development exhibited by students there. Most incoming first-year students exhibit what Fowler (1981) would term the synthetic-conventional faith stage, characterized by religious beliefs that largely conform to the beliefs of others—similar to Kohlberg's (1985) conventional level of morality. This indicates that first-year students at Dordt have not yet adequately analyzed alternative religious ideologies. They do not exhibit a more thoughtful approach to their faith that is the product of deep personal searching, growth, and struggle; rather, they hold to a socially defined faith that reflects their ideological environment. Likewise, most first-year students can be characterized as having a foreclosed status in identity formation, meaning that they tend to accept unquestioningly the expectations of their parents and have not explored their own set of beliefs and vocational choices. As Van Wicklin, Burwell, and Butman (1994) note in their analysis of the data across institutions,

with respect to identity foreclosure, we should keep in mind that it is rather common for a student upon entering college to be foreclosed on parental goals and ideologies. The danger appears to be for those who do not relinquish this pattern of uncritical identification. The longer it remains in place, the greater the likelihood that it will become a terminal as opposed to transitory designation. If Parks (1986) is correct in

asserting that young adulthood is a window of opportunity for identity formation, then those who fail to resolve basic identity issues during the college years are missing a major opportunity to do so. Life circumstances may not be as accommodating in the years to follow. Surely the blame for squandered opportunities does not rest solely with the student. College educators have an ongoing responsibility to know the education process and their clientele well enough to improve the education environment for everyone. (p. 97)

In terms of faith formation, to move to the next stage of development (an individuative/reflective faith) a student must test, consider, and choose a faith and a life course of his or her own, and not simply adopt the prevailing belief systems of the authorities that he or she has trusted up to that point. Such a transition is often born of struggle and conflict, a personal "paradigmatic crisis" which occurs in the life of the young adult as a result of challenging experiences that do not fit neatly into or are not adequately explained by the adopted belief system.

Bussema (1999) found that even though most of the first-year students chose their institution specifically because of the institution's faith commitment orientation, the majority of students who persisted had not clearly moved to a new level of development by their sophomore year. Of those who did move to the next level by their junior or senior year, a common experience emerged in their reflective accounts of their time in college: a significant cross-cultural service-learning endeavor, usually within the sophomore or junior year. Likewise, for those students who clearly moved from foreclosure into moratorium (identity searching and struggle) and through this status into identity achievement, a key aspect was an intercultural service-learning experience that precipitated paradigmatic or personal crisis.

For these students, such experiences often involved forming significant relationships (not necessarily friendships, though often those as well) with those in a different culture who held a very different lifestyle, value system, and/or worldview that challenged the student to reconsider and re-evaluate his or her own paradigm or worldview. Furthermore, if the school orchestrated these significant cross-cultural experiences, making them readily available within the student's major, the developmental impact was even more dramatic because the student could begin to wed existential meaning and transformational educational fulfillment with a clear sense of vocational and career direction and purpose. This process often took the form of a personal belief crisis in the life of the student, from which the student typically emerged with a more thoughtful, reflective, and deeply personal faith commitment—often with the help of a trusted mentor who stood beside the student during this time.

An example of one institution which has carefully integrated all the aspects of transformational education is Spring Arbor College, one of the Templeton honor roll colleges that encourages character development. This school has developed a four-year plan with experiential learning components intended to inspire the student through these developmental progressions. The first-year course intentionally brings students together into small groups that, among other things, begin to challenge them intellectually in examining their worldview, stretch them through "social diversity encounters," and encourage interdependence during a community-building "survival" weekend in the woods of northern Michigan. During the sophomore year, students take a required cross-cultural orientation class that involves a number of simulations, role-playing games meant to enhance inter-cultural sensitivity and awareness, a three-day cultural experiential learning encounter in the ethnic communities and services of Chicago, and a concerted effort to foster a sense of moral and vocational obligation to making a positive difference in a needy world. In their junior

year, students are then required to complete a cross-cultural travel/study option, often involving an emphasis and practicum experience (service learning) in their major field of study. During the senior year, students complete a senior seminar requiring them to develop a final paper and public presentation on the integration of their professional preparation with their worldview and a portfolio recap of the college experiences instrumental in shaping their faith/vocation perspective.

During their senior exit interviews and on their alumni surveys, students at Spring Arbor often note the importance of the cross-cultural experiential learning components in their sophomore and junior years as instrumental in their development as persons. These experiences moved them outside their intellectual and emotional comfort zones. When coupled with skillful faculty mentors in their learning community, such students began to demonstrate growth in achieving intellectual and interpersonal competence, a sense of autonomy and healthy interdependence, identity formation, and a sense of mission and purpose for their lives in the context of their vocations.

In the absence of an intentional program and skillful mentors to enhance such growth, however, students with "paradigm shaking" personal experiences may feel at a loss, uncomfortable and even guilty about questioning what they previously viewed as foundational truths (Loevinger, 1976). During this time, they may desperately look to the "truth seeking" methodologies within their disciplines and broader academic programs. They do so in order to find more robust or vibrant paradigms or worldviews to help them make sense of their experiences and new perspectives. Without the anchor of a mentoring relationship or intentional programmatic "scaffolding," these students often find only more and more (and often redundant) disciplinary content rather than a sense of meaning and purpose. Too often, what we label as a "slump" and view mostly as a problem within the student is actually an outgrowth of trying to find purpose in an environment where they have found no scaffolding and no guides.

Conclusion: Responding to the Sophomore Challenge

Centuries ago, the apprentice lived with the master craftsman and his family, not only learning a trade but also learning a life. While this type of apprenticeship is not always practical, there is merit in faculty going beyond the content of their discipline to actually mentor the student in the methodology of the discipline. The laboratory sciences and the performing and fine arts especially tend to emphasize apprenticeship in the methods of the discipline as well as the content of the discipline. Teacher education programs are becoming more and more that way as they become increasingly "methods-based" in complying with accreditation specifications and requirements. Other, more applied majors, that grant certifications such as medical technology, social work, and addictions counseling, increasingly emphasize methodology as well in their coursework and in their internship and practica requirements.

Programs that have a strong skills or methodology emphasis as they begin to apprentice students within that major during the sophomore year may stave off some elements of the sophomore slump. As students move from a diffuse general education curricular emphasis of the first year (which may have included a well-integrated first-year student experience component) to a methods-based and more focused academic major, they may sense that they are beginning to learn skills in their academic area of interest that will prepare them for future opportunities.

Methodology, skills, and competencies are necessary components which should begin to be built during the sophomore year if not sooner. However, they are meant as a means to an end, the end being equipping students to become educated, thinking, virtuous citizens and caring human beings skilled for a vocation. Educating the virtuous and caring citizen is inextricably linked to ego formation, faith formation, intellectual formation, emotional well-being, psychological well-being, existential well-being, physical health and vitality, and ultimately, moral development (Marcia, 1987).

Sophomore students will find enduring fulfillment within their educational experience if they sense they are achieving some growth in the four areas we have discussed in this chapter: achieving competence, developing autonomy, establishing identity, and developing purpose. If they sense that they are becoming better and more fulfilled human beings as they become better scientists, artists, musicians, or social workers, then their lives will have been transformed by their educational experience. Our colleges and universities have a mandate to foster growth in these students by actively encouraging them to become better human beings and achieve a clearer sense of life purpose or fulfillment. The place to begin is through praxis in the life of the sophomore, gained through significant experiential/cross-cultural learning and processed through meaningful mentoring relationships as a foundation for discipleship or apprenticeship within the discipline.

References

Astin, A. (1993). *What matters in college: Four critical years revisited*. San Francisco: Jossey-Bass.

Banning, J. H. (1989). Impact of college environments on freshman student students. In M. L. Upcraft, J. N. Gardner, & Associates (Eds.), *The freshman year experience* (pp. 53-62). San Francisco: Jossey-Bass.

Barefoot, B. O., & Fidler, P. P. (1996). *The 1994 national survey of freshman seminar programs: Continuing innovations in the collegiate curriculum* (Monograph No. 20). Columbia, SC: University of South Carolina, National Resource Center for The Freshman Year Experience & Students in Transition.

Baylis, B. (1995). Comparison of 1994 freshmen at Christian colleges and universities (CCCU) and students at private, Protestant institutions and at all four-year institutions based on fall 1994 CIRP data. *Research on Christian Higher Education, 2,* 143-165.

Baylis, B. (1996). *Taking values seriously: Assessing the mission of church-related higher education–A review of the first 18 months of the project.* Retrieved from the World Wide Web: http://cccu/news/assess.html

Baylis, B. (1997a). *Taking values seriously: Assessing the mission of church-related higher education–Summary report of the 1995 faculty survey.* Retrieved from the World Wide Web: http://cccu/news/assess.html

Baylis, B. (1997b). *Taking values seriously: Assessing the mission of church-related higher education–1996 report on the CCCU alumni: 1994 graduates of CCCU institutions.* Retrieved from the World Wide Web: http://cccu/news/assess.html

Boivin, M. J. (1988). In memoriam John Lee Allen, Ph.D. *Journal of Psychology and Christianity, 7*(2).

Boivin, M. J., Beuthin, T. M., & Hauger, G., (1993). Why Christian students leave Christian colleges: Evaluating the dynamics of adjustment in a Christian community. *The Journal of the Freshman Year Experience, 5,* 93-125.

Bussema, K. E., (1999). Who am I? Whose am I?: Identity and faith in the college years. *Research in Christian Higher Education, 6,* 1-33.

Butman, R. (1993). The 'critical years' of young adulthood. In K. Gangel & J. Wilhoit (Eds.), *The Christian educator's handbook on adult education* (pp. 247-261). Wheaton, IL: Victor/Scripture Press.

Butman, R. (1999). *Scaffolding in the critical years: Connecting the SOP learning landscapes at Fuller Seminary.* Presentation to the faculty development workshop at Fuller Theological Seminary, Pasadena, CA.

Campolo, T. (1984, Spring). Praxis: The revolutionary new principle for crisis counseling. *Youth Worker,* 48-51.

Chickering, A. W. (1969). *Education and identity.* San Francisco: Jossey-Bass.

Erikson, E. (1968). *Identity: Youth and crisis.* New York: Norton.

Feldman, K. & Newcomb, T. (1969). *The impact of college on students.* San Francisco: Jossey-Bass.

Fowler, J. (1981). *Stages of faith.* San Francisco: Harper and Row.

Garber, S. (1996). *The fabric of faithfulness.* Downer's Grove, IL: InterVarsity.

John Templeton Foundation. (1999). *Colleges that encourage character development: A resource for parents, students, and educators.* Philadelphia, PA: Templeton Foundation Press. Retrieved from the World Wide Web: http://www.templeton.org/Press.colleges_character_develop.asp)

Kohlberg, L. (1985). *The psychology of moral development.* San Francisco: Harper & Row.

Lemons, L. J., & Richmond, D. R. (1987). A developmental perspective of sophomore slump. *NASPA Journal, 24,* 15-19.

Loevinger, J. (1976). *Ego development: Conceptions and theories*. San Francisco: Jossey-Bass.

Marcia, J. (1987). The identity status approach to the study of ego identity development. In T. Honess & K. Yardley (Eds.), *Self and identity: Perspectives across the lifespan* (pp. 161-171). London: Routhledge & Kegan Paul.

Marcus, P. M. (1973). Accountability: Still another point of view. *Planning For Higher Education, 2*(4), 1-4.

Palmer, P. (1998). *The courage to teach: Exploring the inner landscape of a teacher's life*. San Francisco: Jossey-Bass.

Parks, S. (1986). *The critical years: The search for a faith to live by*. San Francisco: Harper Collins.

Pascarella, E. & Terenzini, P. (1991). *How college affects students: Findings and insights from twenty years of research*. San Francisco: Jossey-Bass.

Perry, W. G., Jr. (1970). *Forms of intellectual and ethical development in college*. New York: Holt, Rinehart & Winston.

Perry, W. G., Jr., (1981). Cognitive and ethical growth: The making of meaning. In A. W. Chickering (Ed.), *The modern American college: Responding to the new realities of diverse students and a changing society*. San Francisco: Jossey-Bass.

Schreiner, L. (2000, February). *Advising strategies for sophomore success*. Paper presented at the annual First-Year Experience conference, Columbia, SC.

Van Wicklin, J., Burwell, R., & Butman, R. (1994). Squandered years: Identity foreclosed students and the liberal education they avoid. In J. Lee & G. Stronks (Eds.), *Assessment in Christian higher education: Rhetoric and reality* (pp. 74-102). Washington: University Press of America.

Wilder, J. S. (1993). The sophomore slump: A complex developmental period that contributes to attrition. *College Student Affairs Journal, 12*, 18-27.

Willard, D. (1999, October). *The assessment of faithful change in the academy*. Keynote address to the National Assessment Conference of the Council for Christian Colleges & Universities, Point Loma University, San Diego, CA.

Assessing the Expectations and Satisfaction Levels of Sophomores: *How Are They Unique?*

by Stephanie Juillerat

Chapter 2

One of the primary goals of this monograph is to determine whether sophomores have unique needs and issues that, when ignored, can ultimately lead to a lack of involvement and motivation in college: a phenomenon commonly referred to as the "sophomore slump." Additionally, higher education experts are trying to determine if sophomores require the same, or similar, specialized attention that is given to at-risk, first-year students in order

to prevent sophomores from dropping out of college. The purpose of this chapter is to examine the expectations and satisfaction levels of sophomores to determine their distinct perceptions or levels of satisfaction, so that we can better understand them and meet their needs more effectively.

The data reported in this chapter indicate that while sophomores' experiences and perceptions are similar in many ways to those of other students, several unique perceptions exist.[1] Identifying these perceptions may enable us

to meet sophomores' needs more appropriately, depending on the type of institution the student attends. For example, when comparing the experiences of sophomores on public and private college campuses, public college sophomores place a higher value on specific services (e.g., library staff, quality of instruction in the classroom, financial aid, and food services), yet they are less satisfied with the level of service provided to them in these and other service areas. Private college sophomores, on the other hand, place high value on a great number of issues.

Most important to private college sophomores are issues of safety, quality academic and personal support services, channels for self-expression, and a sense of pride in the campus environment. While not as dissatisfied as juniors and seniors, sophomores are the least satisfied group with regard to some of these same personal and academic issues—issues that directly impact their sense of well-being (e.g., caring, knowledgeable faculty; advisors who are concerned about student success; faculty who give prompt feedback about students' progress; and conflict-free registration).

These distinct issues may highlight a fundamental difference between the needs of sophomores at private and public college settings. The apparent trend is for sophomores in private colleges to have high expectations and to need more care, guidance, and feelings of well-being and belonging. While sophomores at public colleges do not have the same high expectations, they do demand better services and systems to help them accomplish their goals. Meeting the needs of sophomores may require a variety of approaches based on institutional characteristics.

An examination of private college sophomore dropouts reveals several interesting findings. First, sophomore dropouts, as expected, have significantly lower satisfaction scores than sophomore persisters and first-year student dropouts. More surprising, however, is that sophomore dropouts do not fit the same pattern of high expectations that we see in a typical private college sophomore. In fact, dropouts have significantly lower importance scores than sophomore persisters, which may indicate that lowered expectations (or the lack of rising expectations) play a role in the sophomore slump.

This chapter attempts to identify those issues that distinguish sophomores in terms of their college expectations and satisfaction levels.

After describing the instrument used for the analyses and the sample on which they were conducted, this chapter summarizes a number of different comparisons. The first analysis examines what sophomores value most strongly in their college educational experience and with which aspects they are most and least satisfied. Responses of private and public college sophomores are also examined to look for commonalties and noteworthy differences between these two populations. A third analysis compares sophomores at each type of institution to the other three class levels to determine unique issues for sophomores. In addition to determining what makes current college sophomores distinct from other students, the final analysis of this study identifies potential retention issues for sophomores by examining the perceptions of sophomores who have subsequently withdrawn from college. Our goal is to illuminate issues related to the sophomore slump so that appropriate interventions can be made to facilitate sophomores' progression to graduation.

Description of the Study

The Instrument

The survey used to assess levels of expectation and satisfaction in college students was the Student Satisfaction Inventory (SSI) (Schreiner & Juillerat, 1993b). The SSI is a 73-item instrument that assesses a large number of areas related to the college experience. The SSI's scores have demonstrated reliability and validity (Juillerat, 1995; Juillerat, in progress), and over 1000 colleges and universities in the United States are currently using the instrument. The authors of the instrument used some of the major principles of consumer theory as the basis for the SSI's construction. Thus, students are viewed as consumers who have definite expectations about what they want from their college experience. Based on this perspective, satisfaction with college occurs when these expectations are met or exceeded by an institution (Schreiner &

Juillerat, 1993a). Therefore, the SSI investigates both strength of expectations and satisfaction that expectations are being met.

Each item on the SSI is stated as a positive expectation a student may or may not have about campus life or institutional services (e.g., "My academic advisor is concerned about my success as an individual."). For each of the items, respondents are first asked to rate how important the expectation is to their overall satisfaction with college, using a seven-point Likert scale ranging from 1 ("not at all important") to 7 ("very important"). Secondly, respondents are requested to rate their level of satisfaction that the school has met the expectation, using a seven-point Likert scale ranging from 1 ("not at all satisfied") to 7 ("very satisfied"). A "not applicable" option is included for instances when an institution does not offer a particular service or in the event that a student has not encountered some aspect of campus life (e.g., counseling services). Thus, each item generates three scores: an importance score, a satisfaction score, and a gap score that indicates the discrepancy between importance and satisfaction.

The Subjects

This study used the survey responses of 118,706 traditional undergraduate students (72,245 from private colleges and 44,461 from public colleges) who completed the SSI in the 1998-1999 academic year. The sample is evenly distributed between genders (54% women; 46% men) and contains slightly more first-year students (38.4%) than upper-class students (20.1% sophomores, 21.3% juniors, and 20.2% seniors). The sample of students is predominantly Caucasian (70.3%) with only moderate representation from other racial groups (African American, 9.5%; Native American, .8%; Asian, 5%; Hispanic, 5.9%). The majority of the students are enrolled full-time (92.8%) and attend classes during the day (91.8%). When the sample is separated by type of institution (private vs. public), as well

as by class level (first-year student, sophomore, junior, senior), the distribution of demographic characteristics is very similar to those of the entire sample, thereby assuring valid comparisons can be made.

A second study conducted to examine sophomore retention issues used a sample comprised of the responses of 5,926 first-year and sophomore students enrolled at 64 private religiously affiliated colleges who completed the SSI in the fall of 1998. Of these, 811 first-year students and 422 sophomores are identified as dropouts due to their withdrawal from college by the fall of 1999. Some noteworthy differences exist between the samples of these two studies. In this second sample, there are substantially greater numbers of Caucasians (83% compared to 70.3%) and residential students (81% compared to 44.6%); it is also important to note that this second sample consists of students who attended religiously affiliated colleges, a fact that must be considered before making any generalizations about private college dropouts.

The Analyses

In order to answer the question "what makes sophomores unique?", a number of analyses were conducted to compare public and private college sophomores to members of other class levels or groups. In all of these comparisons, one of two basic statistical techniques was used: a comparison of score rankings or a test of statistical differences in score values. The score ranking technique simply compares the rankings of the 73 SSI items by the various groups and looks for similarities and differences in those items that appear at the top and bottom of the importance and satisfaction lists, without any interest in the actual values or scores for the items. The examination of rankings allows us to see differences and similarities in the relative importance or satisfaction of an item, compared to all the other items on the SSI, without looking at how high or low the actual score is. We can get a feel for how important or satisfying an item is, compared to other items.

The second analysis, the test of statistical difference, utilizes either a *t*-test or analysis of variance (ANOVA) to determine if one group's (usually sophomores) score on an item is significantly higher or lower than another group's score on the same item ($p < .05$). Rather than looking at relative position on a list of 73 items, the test of statistical difference looks at the strength of the score that has been assigned to an item. This allows us to determine if sophomores had stronger expectations or levels of satisfaction or dissatisfaction on various items.

While these analyses may sometimes sound similar, they answer two different but equally valuable questions about sophomores. A distinction will be made between the two analyses by referring to "rankings" or "ratings" when discussing items that have been identified by rank comparison and referring to "significant differences" in particular "scores" when discussing items that have been identified through the *t*-test or ANOVA techniques.

Sophomores' Expectations and Satisfaction Levels

Before determining if and in what way sophomores are a unique population, it is important to determine what is most important to them (what they expect), where they are or are not satisfied, and in what ways they are similar to other levels of students.

What Do Sophomores Value in a College Education?

To determine what sophomores value in a college education, one only needs to look at the items that sophomores rank as most important on the SSI. These items fall into the following categories:

- An environment that promotes intellectual growth
- Valuable course content and excellent classroom instruction
- Knowledgeable, fair, and caring faculty
- Approachable and knowledgeable advisors
- Tuition that is a worthwhile investment
- Adequate financial aid
- A smooth registration process with a good variety of courses offered
- An enjoyable experience being a student

With few exceptions, these are the same issues that first-year students, juniors, and seniors rank as most important at both private and public colleges. But while the predominant characteristics that sophomores value in their college experience are no different from those valued by other students, sophomores' expectation levels begin to differ substantially from other class levels once we get beyond what is valued most. These differences will be discussed shortly.

What Issues Impact Sophomores' Levels of Satisfaction?

It is encouraging that a large number of the items ranked as most important to sophomores (as well as students of other class levels) are also the items ranked as the most satisfying (with the exception of financial aid, registration processes, and worthwhile tuition). In addition, the areas in which sophomores express the least satisfaction (lowest rankings) tend to be the same areas with which other class levels express dissatisfaction as well: (a) non-academic service issues, such as reasonable billing policies, adequate financial aid, appropriate activities fees and tuition, adequate information sharing (not getting the run-around), and adequate health services; and (b) issues affecting their lives as students on campus, such as weekend activities, athletic programs, food services, parking, residence hall rules, and channels for expressing complaints. However, there are some notable areas where sophomores express greater levels of dissatisfaction than any other class level on campus, and these will be discussed later.

Public versus Private College Sophomores

Another consideration that must be addressed before we begin to discuss issues related specifically to the sophomore slump is whether or not the issues of private college sophomores are the same as those of public college sophomores. Do both groups have the same expectations and satisfaction levels, or is there a systematic difference between the two populations? Examining the data from the SSI reveals some definite similarities, along with some noteworthy differences, between the two groups.

Typically, when comparing private and public college sophomores, the rankings of what is most important and most and least satisfying are quite similar. Where public college sophomores appear to be different from private college sophomores in terms of importance score rankings is in their higher relative ranking of the importance of faculty availability, adequate student parking, and reasonable billing policies. Private college sophomores appear to be different from those at public colleges in their higher relative ranking of the importance of issues of adequate financial aid, having an enjoyable campus experience, and having a commitment to academic excellence (See Table 1 in Appendix A). In terms of satisfaction score rankings, public college sophomores are relatively more satisfied with the variety of courses, helpfulness of library and bookstore staff, and adequacy of library resources. Private college sophomores are relatively more satisfied with the caring nature of campus staff, being made to feel welcome, and the commitment to academic excellence. Most noteworthy when looking at the least satisfying rankings of these two groups is that private college sophomores rank the value of tuition much lower in their list than do sophomores in public colleges (See Table 2 in Appendix A).

Although agreement exists on many of the items considered the most and least important and satisfying in the college experience, one notable difference is that the private college sophomore often identifies those experiences as both more important and more satisfying by assigning higher scores to those items. Although higher importance scores in private college sophomores are a fairly consistent trend, there are several areas which are significantly more important to the public college sophomore when the actual scores are compared.

These include student parking, advising experiences, health services, variety of courses offered, intramural sports, helpfulness of library staff, and a conflict-free registration process (See Table 1 in Appendix A). And while private college sophomores tend to be more satisfied than sophomores at public colleges, there are some exceptions to this trend as well. Areas where private college sophomores are significantly less satisfied than sophomores at public colleges include library resources and services, athletics and intramural sports, variety of courses offered, adequacy of computer labs, value of tuition, selection of food available, quality of the student center, and protection of students' freedom of expression (See Table 2 in Appendix A).

It is evident that sophomores at public colleges have some different issues than their private college counterparts, and these unique issues are lost when the data are combined. Therefore, throughout this chapter, all further analyses will investigate the two types of students separately, and any commonalties or differences will be noted accordingly.

Class Level Differences for Sophomores

In order to explore the notable differences between sophomores and students at other class levels, the importance and satisfaction scores of sophomores at each type of college were compared to other class levels of students on those same campuses using an ANOVA, to determine if sophomores as a class had significantly different perceptions.

Private College Sophomore Differences

Differences in importance scores. Of the 73 SSI items that were compared across class levels, sophomores had the strongest levels of expectation (highest importance score) on 17 of them. They shared the highest importance scores with another class on 11 additional items, and they had significantly higher scores than both juniors and seniors on an additional 17 items. All told, sophomores had significantly higher expectations from another class level on over half the items on the SSI (See Table 3 in Appendix A).

The areas receiving higher importance scores from sophomores than from any other class level include feeling a sense of belonging and pride, reasonable add/drop policies, and the fairness of student disciplinary procedures. Additional items emerge as significant for sophomores when we look at importance scores that increase significantly from the first year of college. These include:

- Campus life issues—adequate residence hall rules and living conditions, caring resident hall staff, sufficient number of weekend activities, equal opportunities to participate in sports, and opportunities for campus involvement
- Staff services—effectiveness of counseling staff, security personnel, tutoring, and career services
- Financial aid issues
- Opportunities for intellectual growth
- Approachable administrators and faculty who are available outside of class
- Freedom of expression and channels for student complaints
- Safety and security issues
- Campus climate issues

Differences in satisfaction scores. The trend that emerges when comparing sophomores'

satisfaction scores to those of students at different class levels is consistent with a pattern of decreasing satisfaction with college. That is, first-year students are typically most satisfied with their college experiences, followed by sophomores and juniors, with seniors being the least satisfied overall. However, there are four interesting instances when sophomores are significantly less satisfied than the students in other class levels. These differences may very well be contributing to the sophomore slump that has been described by Pattengale and Schreiner elsewhere in this monograph. Perhaps most noteworthy is that sophomores are significantly less satisfied than all other students with the approachability and concern of their advisors, issues they have already identified as being critically important to them. Sophomores are also significantly less satisfied with the registration process being free of scheduling conflicts and with receiving timely feedback from faculty in a course. Finally, sophomores are the least satisfied with the caring nature of faculty members, although not to a statistically significant degree. All of these items paint a picture congruent with the idea that the academic component of a sophomore's experience, and especially the caring nature of college faculty, somehow becomes less satisfying, which is particularly damaging given the importance they place on these components, as measured by the SSI (See Table 4 in Appendix A).

Public College Sophomore Differences

Differences in importance scores. The importance scores among public college students tend to flow in a sequential order, either beginning with first-year students having the lowest importance scores and moving systematically higher, or with first-year students having the highest importance scores and moving systematically lower across class levels. Sophomores and juniors rarely have the highest importance scores (See Table 5 in Appendix A).

Most noteworthy to this discussion is that public college sophomores have the highest importance scores on far fewer items than their private college counterparts. In fact, there are only seven items where sophomores have the highest importance score of all class levels. These items address issues related to financial aid and billing policies, as well as the approachability of administrators and faculty who are considerate of student differences. In other cases, while first-year students have the highest importance scores, sophomores have significantly higher importance scores than both juniors and seniors on items related to campus life (sports, residence halls, food services, organizations, and activities), tutoring, and career services; and they place a greater value on access to information. All in all, however, it appears as if public college sophomores do not have the unusually high expectations that private college sophomores do, which results in fewer distinctions between public college sophomores and students at other class levels.

Differences in satisfaction scores. Sophomores had the lowest satisfaction scores among public college students on only four items. These include the helpfulness of library staff, excellent instruction in the major, adequate financial aid, and an adequate selection of food in the cafeteria. In most cases, the juniors and seniors are far less satisfied than the first-year students or sophomores, a trend that is consistent across all types of colleges. However, it is important to note that public college sophomores have the highest importance scores and the lowest satisfaction levels regarding financial aid, which may indicate an important issue that institutions need to address (See Table 6 in Appendix A).

Sophomore Retention Issues

One of the best ways to identify issues related to the sophomore slump is to examine the opinions of sophomores who have already "slumped" (to the point of withdrawing from college). The SSI responses of 5,926 first-year students and sophomores who attended 64 private, religiously-affiliated liberal arts colleges were analyzed to determine if the issues related to sophomore attrition could be accurately identified. Of the students in this sample, 811 first-year students and 422 sophomores were identified as dropouts due to their withdrawal from college within a year of completing the SSI.

Differences Between Sophomore Dropouts and Persisters

One useful way of determining the retention issues of sophomores is to compare the expectations and satisfaction levels of sophomores who persisted to those of sophomores who subsequently withdrew from the college. This approach differs from most retention research (e.g., Astin, 1993; Tinto, 1987) in that the responses were acquired from the students almost a year before any decision was made to stay or leave the institution. In this way, we can determine if there are significant differences in their perceptions before those perceptions were colored by the decision to leave the institution.

A *t*-test comparison of 422 sophomore dropouts and 2,118 sophomore persisters reveals a number of significant differences between the two groups. Interestingly, sophomore dropouts have lower importance scores on every item, but the lower scores are statistically significant on only 26 of the 73 items. These 26 items address issues of campus climate, advising, staff helpfulness, faculty and instructional effectiveness, safety and security, financial aid, registration processes, and the library resources—virtually all of which rate among the top items that are most important to students regardless of their class level. This would seem to indicate that the higher expectations identified previously as characteristic of sophomores are not at issue for those who drop out. In fact, the reverse seems to be the case, in that the sophomores with the lower expectations are the at-risk group.

While the differences in importance scores are statistically significant on only about one-third of the items, a *t*-test comparison of the satisfaction scores of these two groups reveals that the sophomore dropouts are significantly less satisfied than the persisters on all but three items on the SSI: (a) the helpfulness of library staff, (b) the registration personnel, and (c) the institution's commitment to students with disabilities. The areas where sophomore dropouts' satisfaction levels are most significantly lower than sophomore persisters' are as follows (for each of these, dropouts' satisfaction scores are at least .50 lower than persisters' scores):

- Enjoy being a student
- Tuition is a worthwhile investment
- Feeling a sense of pride about the campus
- Variety of courses offered
- Student activity fees put to good use
- Living conditions in the residence halls
- Course content in the major
- Residence hall regulations
- Fair student disciplinary procedures

From this analysis, the data seem to suggest that sophomore dropouts' lowered expectations and decreased satisfaction levels play an important role in their decision to withdraw.

Differences Between First-Year Students and Sophomore Dropouts

Another key question to be answered about sophomore attrition data is whether or not the picture is any different from first-year student attrition. A *t*-test comparison of the 422 sophomore dropouts to the 811 first-year student dropouts reveals that sophomore dropouts have the highest importance scores on every item on the SSI, yet have significantly higher importance scores than first-year students on only 23 of the SSI items, indicating that while many expectations rise even among those who eventually leave the institution, the higher expectations may not be the critical retention issue.

In addition, sophomore dropouts have lower satisfaction scores than first-year student dropouts on all but six of the SSI items, yet those differences are statistically significant on only 36 of the SSI items. These 36 areas encompass financial issues, campus "run-around," service excellence, maintenance, staff issues, library resources, courses offered, registration processes, the value of tuition, issues of faculty fairness, and a number of student life issues.

The only item where sophomore dropouts are significantly more satisfied than first-year student dropouts is: "My academic advisor is knowledgeable about requirements in my major." Thus the pattern of decreasing satisfaction from the first-year student to the sophomore year that we see in all students is also seen in those students who eventually leave an institution. The top areas where sophomore dropouts' satisfaction levels are most significantly lower than first-year student dropouts' satisfaction levels are as follows (differences of .40 or higher):

- Library resources and services
- Campus "run-around"
- Financial aid issues
- Variety of courses offered
- Billing policies and fees
- Staff in the health services area
- Student center
- Registration processes
- Channels for student complaints
- Commitment to commuters
- Tuition as a worthwhile investment

Before making any generalizations from this study to the larger population of sophomore dropouts, it is important to be aware that the sample was drawn entirely from private colleges with a religious affiliation and is not, therefore, representative of all sophomores.

Concluding Remarks

Drawing conclusions from the data of thousands of students who have given their perceptions of almost a hundred aspects of their campus experience can be a difficult and confusing endeavor. To summarize what this research has found so far:

1. When assessing what sophomores value most about their college experience, few differences are found between sophomores and other class levels. All students rate as most important a climate of intellectual growth; excellent instruction; knowledgeable, fair, and caring faculty; tuition that is worthwhile; and adequate financial aid. And all students—sophomores included—are most satisfied with knowledgeable and available faculty, caring staff, and being made to feel welcome. Students are least satisfied with financial issues (e.g., billing, financial aid, appropriate fees and tuition), getting the run-around, and issues related to campus life (e.g., food services, parking, residence hall rules, weekend activities).

2. In general, private college sophomores have significantly stronger expectations (higher importance scores) and higher levels of satisfaction than sophomores attending public colleges. Exceptions are in the areas of athletics, computer resources, food services, student center, value of tuition, and variety of courses offered, where private college sophomores have significantly lower levels of satisfaction than their counterparts at public colleges.

3. Private college sophomores have or share the highest expectation levels on 28 SSI items and have significantly higher expectations than juniors and seniors on 17 additional items. Expectations that distinguish private college sophomores include a number of areas related to a safe, involving, and fair campus life; effective staff; tutoring services; adequate financial aid; and freedom of expression. The few items where private college sophomores are significantly less satisfied than other class levels address advising, faculty feedback about course progress, and conflict-free registration.

4. Public college sophomores have significantly higher importance scores than first-year students or seniors in areas related to financial aid, billing, and faculty consideration of student differences; and they have significantly higher importance scores than juniors and seniors on a number of campus life issues, tutoring, and career services. Like their private college counterparts, public college sophomores are significantly less satisfied than first-year students, juniors, and seniors on very few items (library staff helpfulness, quality of instruction, adequate financial aid, and food services); however, financial aid is an issue that consistently arises for public college sophomores.

5. In general, sophomores at both types of institutions seem to place more value (higher importance) on the admissions, financial aid and registration services, residence hall issues, tutoring and career services, being involved, and feeling a sense of belonging on campus. Private college sophomores have significantly more items that distinguish them from other class levels than their public college counterparts. They place particular importance on being able to voice their opinions and having fair disciplinary procedures on campus.

6. The issues that are significantly less satisfying to sophomores differ based on type of institution. Sophomores at private colleges are much less satisfied with the approachability, knowledge, and caring nature of faculty and advisors, as well as the registration process being free of conflicts, while sophomores at public colleges are much less satisfied with the library staff service, selection of food, quality of instruction, and financial aid.

7. Sophomore dropouts, at least in the sample studied, have somewhat lower expectations and significantly lower satisfaction scores than sophomore persisters. Perhaps their lower expectations signal their disengagement or lack of connection to the

institution, even when assessed almost a year before leaving. Lower expectations could also indicate a lack of familiarity with the college experience or the institution. We could even hypothesize that the lower expectations are a reflection of the motivational "slump" seen in some sophomores—indicative of a general apathy toward college. Sophomore dropouts are particularly less satisfied with enjoying being a student, the value of tuition, feeling a sense of pride about their campus, the variety of courses offered, student activity fees, living conditions in the residence halls, regulations and disciplinary procedures, and the course content in their major.

8. Sophomore dropouts in this sample have significantly higher importance scores than first-year student dropouts on about one-third of the SSI items and are significantly less satisfied than first-year student dropouts on about half of the items on the SSI. They are particularly less satisfied than first-year student dropouts are with library resources and services, getting the campus "run-around," the timing and adequacy of financial aid awards and the helpfulness of financial aid counselors, billing policies, health services, variety of courses offered, the student center, registration processes, channels for student complaints, institutional commitment to commuters, and tuition as a worthwhile investment.

When we consider the trends discussed in this article, it becomes readily apparent that there are distinctive issues and needs related to the sophomore experience, many of which may be contributing to the sophomore slump. For public college sophomores, who value hassle-free service and excellent instruction, institutions need to examine their policies and procedures, as well as the level of service offered to sophomores, to determine what changes need to be made to enable sophomores to have a high-quality educational experience. For example, financial aid issues are extremely important to public college sophomores and represent one area

where colleges should examine policies and procedures.

For private college sophomores, who have a large number of high expectations and a need to feel care and concern, colleges need to examine the quality of their programming for sophomores, as well as the level of care and concern demonstrated toward them by all campus constituents. Given that private college sophomores have the highest expectations on so many items, one approach that must be considered is whether these high expectations are in line with reality. Simply put, sophomores may have unreasonably high expectations regarding some of the services on campus.

These high expectations may develop from a number of experiences, including promises made during recruitment, the level of service they received as first-year students, perceived better treatment of juniors or seniors, or any number of other influences. Regardless of the source, the high expectations need to be evaluated to determine if they are unreasonably high, or if they are legitimately high given the promises an institution is making. On the other hand, these high expectations may be a reflection of the student's commitment to the institution, since the private college sophomores who drop out are likely to have lower importance scores than those who persist. Our institutions may also need to have greater concern for sophomores with lower expectations and a sense of gratitude to those with higher expectations!

Assuming that sophomore expectations are realistic—or at least adaptive—something must be done to address the apparent negative feelings that private college sophomores have concerning their well-being and care, especially in the academic advising process. Perhaps students who seek out a private college environment need or expect more personal attention as part of the educational process, which is why sophomores may often feel disenchanted or ignored when they return from the first year. As Pattengale and Schreiner aptly point out in this monograph, colleges offer a variety of specialized programs, developed and implemented for first-year students, to get students through the first college year. Perhaps the lack of this specialized attention in the sophomore year has a more damaging impact to private college sophomores than first imagined because of the importance private college students place on personalized attention—an expectation they may have formed because of the recruiting materials provided by many private colleges that promote the idea of individual attention and student-centeredness. It may be that the sophomore year is too early to wean students off the specialized attention they were receiving as first-year students, because it is obviously still very important to them. It appears as if private college sophomores need the special programs to continue, while public college sophomores just want a hassle-free experience.

Decreased satisfaction has been linked quite convincingly to the dropout process, especially when the lower satisfaction levels are in areas related to their enjoyment of life as a student and with their academic experience. As we often see in families, the cries for attention from the "middle child" often get lost amidst the clamorings of the younger and older siblings (who have many legitimate needs of their own). As a result, middle children may feel like the rest of the family does not care or cannot attend to their needs. In the case of higher education, it may be that our best efforts to provide care and service are driven by the most urgent needs: getting our first-year students started off on the right track and making sure that our soon-to-be alumni have all the tools they need for a successful career and a fond remembrance of their alma mater.

These best efforts need to be extended to the "middle children," who may have gotten off to a good start, but who may never reach alumni status if they are not better nurtured and better served.

Notes

[1] Please refer to Appendix A for detailed statistical analysis.

References

Astin, A. (1993). *What matters in college? Four critical years revisited.* San Francisco: Jossey-Bass.

Juillerat, S. (1995). *Investigating a two-dimensional approach to the assessment of student satisfaction: Validation of the student satisfaction inventory* (Doctoral dissertation, Temple University).

Juillerat, S. (in progress). Using quality principles in the assessment of college student satisfaction: Validation of the Student Satisfaction Inventory. Paper submitted for publication to *Educational and Psychological Measurement.*

Schreiner, L. A., & Juillerat, S. L. (1993a, July). *Closing the gap between expectation and reality: The key to student satisfaction.* Paper presented at the Noel/Levitz Conference on Student Retention, New Orleans.

Schreiner, L. A., & Juillerat, S. L. (1993b). *The student satisfaction inventory.* Iowa City, IA: Noel/Levitz Centers, Inc.

Tinto, V. (1987). *Leaving college.* Chicago: The University of Chicago Press.

Policies And Practices To Enhance Sophomore Success

by Jerry Pattengale

Chapter 3

Since 1998, the editors of this monograph have explored the phenomenon of the sophomore slump in national and regional conference sessions. These sessions have engaged educators in conversations centered on the same series of questions from which many common themes emerged. Through these conference sessions and numerous on-campus consulting trips, we have gleaned a variety of examples of how some institutions are already

meeting the unique needs of second-year students. In addition to a summary of the key issues, concerns, and responses revealed in these sessions, this chapter begins with the research context and concludes with a section on existing programs attempting to address sophomore issues.

Few resources on sophomore issues and strategies exist, and we hope this monograph will prompt numerous studies and articles to expand the knowledge base in this area. Other than a dissertation on sophomore retention (Flanagan 1990), which includes less than a dozen sources addressing sophomore issues, most of the attention paid to the

sophomore year has been generally descriptive in nature. Little research has targeted sophomores as a unique population. In order to provide as broad a coverage of this topic as possible for this monograph, the editors conducted numerous telephone interviews, listserv conversations, and extended dialogues with interested scholars to produce the sources and examples that appear in this chapter and throughout the monograph.

In light of the paucity of resources available and the clamor for answers to sophomore issues, the leaders of the National Resource Center for The First-Year Experience and

Students in Transition at the University of South Carolina initiated this project with the purpose of helping the academy deal with an important group of often-neglected students—sophomores. While the Center has already devoted two decades to refining the education of first-year students, and has very recently given attention to seniors, this is the first concerted effort to deal with the issues surrounding the sophomore year.

The Background of the Problem

Institutions tend to lose half as many students in each subsequent year of enrollment as they do from the first to the second year. This phenomenon, aptly called the "retention funnel" (Figure 1), has been popularized by Lee Noel and Randi Levitz (1991). The funnel metaphor suggests that if an institution has a 56.5% four-year graduation rate, it likely saw an attrition of 25% of first-year students, 12.5% of sophomores, and 6% of juniors. A 10-year, longitudinal study at the University of Nevada, Reno and Pittsburgh State University (KS) reflects this funnel, with

the exception of the attrition of out-of-state students (Davidson & Muse, 1994).

Yet this expected attrition rate does not describe all institutions. A survey of 65 private institutions associated with the Council of Christian Colleges and Universities (CCCU) revealed that 40.6% of the students left before their junior year, yet only 24.1% of the students left before their sophomore year. This is a sizable deviation from the expected rate of attrition. Similarly, Flanagan's (1990) study of 26 selective colleges in the Associated Colleges of the Midwest and of the Great Lakes Colleges Association actually found higher levels of attrition from the sophomore to the junior year than had been seen after the first year.

His study revealed that these colleges, in placing a priority on first-year retention, had endorsed the "front loading" approach, failing to continue student success strategies into the sophomore year. Echoing Tinto (1987), Flanagan (1990) concludes his study by encouraging these colleges to focus on the

Figure 1
The Retention Funnel

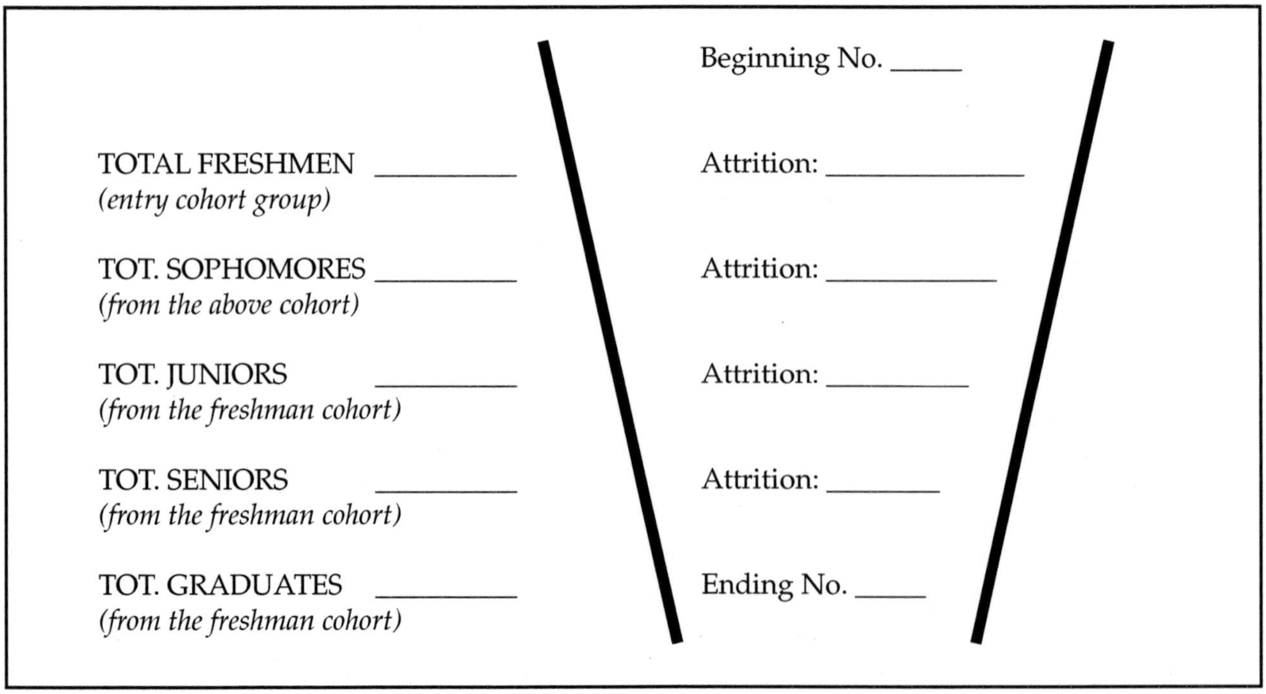

TOTAL FRESHMEN _____
(entry cohort group)

TOT. SOPHOMORES _____
(from the above cohort)

TOT. JUNIORS _____
(from the freshman cohort)

TOT. SENIORS _____
(from the freshman cohort)

TOT. GRADUATES _____
(from the freshman cohort)

Beginning No. _____

Attrition: _____

Attrition: _____

Attrition: _____

Attrition: _____

Ending No. _____

inclusion and developmental needs of sophomore students.

While the national retention funnel percentages might resonate with the numbers on many campuses, the issues of various sophomore cohort groups will likely complicate an interpretation. In her work entitled "The Sophomore Slump: A Complex Developmental Period that Contributes to Attrition," Joyce S. Wilder (1993) found factors other than academic motivation at play among the attriters. Academic abilities and motivation did not explain the significant differences between those who departed and those who stayed among the 192 sophomores she studied.

An increasing number of institutions report that a disproportionate percentage of sophomores fail to return for their junior years. Flanagan found the retention concerns of 26 selective liberal arts colleges were actually more acute during the sophomore year than the first year (Flanagan, 1990; Flanagan, 2000). Without a doubt, sophomore attrition has an impact on graduation rates. According to ACT, Inc. (2000), the five-year graduation rates for four-year colleges in 1999 reached a record low of 51.6% (42.2% and 55.8% respectively for public and private schools), continuing a trend that began in 1996. Likewise, the three-year graduation rate at two-year institutions has steadily decreased since 1992, reaching a record low of 37.5% in 1999.

Educators have attempted to identify this type of recurring phenomenon and have loosely dubbed it "the sophomore slump." Definitions for the sophomore slump vary, and whether it is actually a slump (or more or less severe) is also debated. However, discussions of sophomore issues generally focus on a serious loss of students and similar themes, such as those ferreted out by the editors during national conference sessions. A survey of 670 Penn State sophomores in 1998 illuminated the discussion by giving some common characteristics of the sophomore slump (Moore, 1998 & 2000):

- Burnout
- Sick of the same thing
- Too used to the routine
- Begin to slack off
- Not getting anywhere with your goals
- Difficult to keep motivated
- Tired of working so hard
- Excitement over
- Nothing's new
- A dead zone
- Real life is sneaking up
- Caught between directions
- Don't know which path to choose
- Want to hurry up/graduate
- Think you know it all
- High expectations failing now
- A lot tougher
- Not in academic groove
- Cumulative grade point average (GPA) drops
- Feel invisible
- Not the youngest so not getting the attention, but also not the oldest so not given the opportunities

The above characteristics may reflect deeper systemic problems in institutional programming. In the discussions below, "sophomore" refers to second-year students, whether at two-year or four-year institutions. And, "slump" refers to the dynamics associated with the high attrition of students—either during the sophomore year or as a result of that year. The following responses, and numerous discussions throughout the monograph, reflect a "slump" that is as much a developmental dynamic as it is quantifiable in retention charts. Lemons and Richards (1987) define the sophomore slump as a "period of developmental confusion," and it is often linked to developing competence, autonomy, and purpose and establishing identity (Chickering, 1969).

The comments below reflect an interest among institutions in facilitating sophomore success, while a gap persists between institutional interests and the reality of overall response. As the comments suggest, sophomores are going through a transition as severe, if not more so, than first-year students. These students no longer have the first-year support group, or what Margolis (1976) terms the "fabricated society" (p. 134). Barry Smith's (Vice President for Student Affairs at Roberts Wesleyan College) study (in process) of sophomores at seven select private universities, to be released in Spring 2001, intends to help shed light on the characteristics of persisting sophomores.[1]

Perspectives from Professionals

In the national conversations on this issue, the editors asked participants a series of questions. We have categorized their responses as academic, developmental, and institutional in order to highlight common themes. Overall, we heard much more concern for developmental issues than for those of an academic nature. This emphasis surfaced at every conference in both the intensity and quantity of answers. The questions and answers are listed below:

Q. Why do you think students leave between the sophomore and junior years when they did not leave after the first year?

Academic:
- Not admitted into their major or professional program (lack of satisfactory academic progress)
- Lack of desired academic majors (most significant among the private college sector)
- More difficult curriculum (e.g., the more challenging general education courses are delayed until the second year)
- Increased competition for grades
- Tougher academic standards and heavier workloads
- Sophomore curriculum is often heavy on the core (many students realize a need to take specific core courses as major prerequisites)
- Forced to commit to a major too early—become disenchanted or disinterested

- No "Plan B" when grades slide
- Scholarship loss
- No wonder of learning

Developmental:
- Marriage or significant other elsewhere (women tend to leave)
- Uncertain about their major, career, life goals
- The institution has been either too intrusive or not intrusive enough
- Maturity crisis
- Cost/benefit ratio—"it's just not worth it!"
- Not invested in the institution
- Why am I really here? (family pressure in conflict with student goals/desires)
- Never intended to graduate (most significant among the private college sector)
- Lose academic focus (too comfortable)
- Honeymoon is over
- Lack of support (institutional attention or relatives)
- Co-curricular issues, e.g., lack of involvement and/or chance for leadership
- Parental wishes
- Professional identity crisis—a full-time student with no vocational plans
- Lack of vocational passion

Institutional:
- They have not yet connected to the institution
- Spiritual or mission fit (Most significant among the private college sector)
- Pressure about a major—cost/benefit ratio
- Cumulative effect of a series of bad experiences that have not yet been offset by positive ones
- They are "trading up" after spending two years at a lower cost, "easier," or lower prestige institution (Abeline Christian, for example, realizes up to 20% attrition by the junior year to Texas A & M.)
- Not supportive of academic at-risk after first year
- Financial aid mismanagement (still need help)
- Housing shifts, loss of community sense

- Posting of degree
- Poor academic fit (career guidance lacking)
- Academic weeding (the student's disappointment)
- Can only afford two years (most significant among the private college sector)
- Housing issues
- Cost/benefit study of new sophomore programs

Q. What are the major issues, needs, and/or tasks of sophomores?

Academic:
- Dealing with an intensified curriculum
- Being in an academic twilight zone—not yet fully into the courses in their major, taking mostly general education courses, but not getting the benefit of first-year experience programming and services
- Encountering highly competitive majors and realizing they do not have what it takes to excel—failure to have a "Plan B" ready
- Romantic image of college and college life is dead—reality hits hard
- Second-year "freshman"
- The sophomore year is often a weeding process by professors—selecting the best for the major

Developmental:
- Trying to figure out why they are in college and why they should stay at this one
- Identity crisis—who am I and why am I here?
- Assuming responsibility for self and making decisions becomes even more important, yet not as much attention is given by the institution, so resources may not be used
- Need special emphasis on advising and career planning
- Any negative behavioral patterns from the first year begin to have real consequences on grades or ability to stay in school
- Family crises may occur—parents divorce,

role reversal with parents, etc.
- Peer issues change—relationship with significant other may become more important, friendships solidify (If significant other or best friend becomes disillusioned with the institution, it may affect the student more.)
- Financial needs may change—did not maintain the GPA as a first-year to keep scholarships, parents divorced, other changes
- Incongruence between personal goals and institutional goals
- If the dream is not stronger than the struggle, students are going to quit
- Everything seems relative; few definitive answers exist.
- Cannot get into major and do not know what else to do
- Family crisis as reality of student independence sets in

Institutional:
- Career issues—tension with parents over selecting a major, pressure from the college or friends to pick a major, disillusionment with the major they may have chosen at entrance
- Getting involved on campus
- Institution relaxes its concern from the first year because it has retained these students as sophomores—students may feel let down at the lack of interest the institution now has for them
- The major does not pick up where first-year programs left off, or if it does, it does not do it in the same way
- We have only forestalled attrition crisis for one year with first-year programs

Q. What can/should institutions be doing to help sophomores to persist to graduation?

Academic:
- Create a sophomore orientation program in each major
- Provide ongoing academic support for sophomores
- Use practica and internship experiences to

jump-start passion
- Emphasize the relevance of general education

Developmental:
- Target sophomores for faculty mentoring, especially on faith development (in private colleges) or self-awareness issues
- Provide leadership practica for sophomores
- Help students develop a vision for the future (most significant among the private college sector)
- Implement a sophomore course using junior and senior teaching assistants

Institutional:
- Developmental academic advising targeted to sophomore needs
- Find ways of connecting sophomores more strongly to their majors
- Communicate expectations about the sophomore year to students and families
- Target sophomores for responsible work-study jobs on campus, so students can learn decision-making skills and take personal responsibility. Be sure training is provided
- Use technology for the institution to keep in touch with sophomores—listservs, e-mail, etc.
- Maintain the support provided in the first year, especially for those students who are struggling academically
- Encourage faculty to involve sophomores in undergraduate research
- Encourage service learning in the sophomore curriculum (e.g., mentoring children at the local elementary school, tutoring inner-city kids after school, or other opportunities that are tied into specific courses or majors)
- Focus on co-op education for sophomores, and find ways of getting them into local agencies and businesses to apply what they are learning in their major courses
- Target specific co-curricular activities to sophomore needs

- Add junior/senior teaching assistants to sophomore courses so they witness role models of successful persistence
- Encourage sophomores to participate in a cross-cultural experience (e.g., semester abroad, inner city service-learning project, ethnic religious gathering, etc.)
- Encourage high levels of faculty interaction targeted to sophomores
- Implement a yearlong planning process

Q. What research needs to be done with sophomores?

- Each institution should interview or survey its new junior-transfer students, and ask:
- Why did you choose to come here?
- Why did you leave your previous institution?
- How did your previous institution NOT meet your needs?
- What do you expect from us?
- What is most important to you in an educational institution?
- Climate research—focus groups with sophomores about their perceptions of the campus climate
- Advising research—compare sophomores' perceptions to those of other students; needs assessment
- Compare advising centers to faculty models, looking specifically at sophomores
- Compare sophomores who stay enrolled to those who leave the institution to determine how they differ
- Retention tracking
- Sophomore focus groups
- Profile the persisters (by ethnic, major, socio-economic status, etc.)

Sophomore Programming: What Some Institutions Are Doing

A variety of programs targeting sophomores' needs are already in place across the country. The following examples provide a glimpse of these different approaches to assisting with sophomore success. The essence of many of the above responses can be found embedded in many of these programs.

The examples are divided between academic and developmental foci, with the understanding that many of the programs overlap both areas. The institutional focus is omitted, assuming that an institutional commitment is needed for programs to have been implemented. Program directors of these and other initiatives have welcomed dialogue about intervention and prevention strategies. Readers are encouraged to consult with the staff of the highlighted programs for their own strategic planning.

Addressing Academic Concerns

The University of Indianapolis (Smyth, 2000) requires all full-time students of sophomore standing (those who have earned 26 credit hours but fewer than 60 credit hours) to participate in its Lecture/Performance Series.[2] This one-credit-hour series is part of the liberal arts program at the university and provides an opportunity for students to attend programs of intellectual and/or cultural significance outside the normal classroom setting. Various types of offerings accommodate the students' schedule. Several 50-minute events are scheduled on Tuesday or Thursday afternoons, and a variety of other events are scheduled at other times ranging from one to three hours.

Spartanburg Methodist College (1999) has attempted to ease the transition between the first and second years by extending its College 101 series across three semesters. The sequence includes College 101, 102, and 103—the latter occurring during the fall of the sophomore year. "College 103: The Sophomore Experience" meets formally only a few times and emphasizes campus-wide, cultural, and traditional events. The stated purpose of the course is to help students become more aware of themselves, their capabilities, and their limitations and to them help clarify their

personal values, needs, and attitudes. The course is also intended to introduce students to a diversity of people, cultures, and ideas and to develop appreciation of diversity. Students must attend at least four sessions in three categories of events. Category A is Campus-Wide and Cultural Events. Topics include a wide range of learning experiences, from institutional history to music and dance performances. Category B encompasses the Sophomore Experience Class Sessions, where topics include: Course Orientation, Population in South Carolina, Folk Music Classics, Wofford Presidential Scholar, Transfer Issues, and Holiday Tales. Category C is appropriately entitled Student's Choice and includes a wide variety of selections. Chapel services (limited to three), concerts, art exhibits, plays, and special lectures are options in this category.

The Chemistry and Biochemistry Department at *Beloit College* (WI) offers a special course for sophomores. Beloit's sophomore programming is discussed in more detail below. *Eastern College* also has sophomore courses and is mentioned in Chapter 4. In some disciplines, the sophomore curriculum is receiving special attention for another reason—it may prove to be the most difficult of all four years. At *Westminster College* (MO), the academic writing course is taken during the spring of the sophomore year. This is the final step toward preparation of the portfolio—used for the students' development and institutional assessment (Blair, 1994). Some schools provide students feedback options that usually offer candid appraisals of sophomore curricular strategies, e.g., the Columbia Underground Listing of Professor Ability (CULPA) discussion of core classes (http://www.cumb.org/culpa/core.html).

Southwest Texas State University (STSU) and *Indiana Wesleyan University* (IWU) use sophomores as facilitators in first-year classes. At STSU, the volunteer facilitators are generally academically talented students who have completed the course successfully. IWU also uses sophomore facilitators, but these students are awarded small stipend ($300 for each of the 30 student facilitators). D. S. Johnson and Russell B. Hodges (1990) of STSU note that two assumptions underlie the use of student facilitators: "Many students admitted to college possess the intellectual ability but lack the maturity and discipline to help them successfully prioritize competing demands during this first year on campus; using facilitators as role models gives such students a peer to follow and provides a powerful avenue of communication which the instructor may not possess." Numerous conference presentations and considerable student success literature support peer leadership. At IWU, one of the highest ranked aspects of the first-year course was its use of peer leaders (Bence, 2000).

Stanford University (CA) uses its Sophomore College program to assist a select diverse group of sophomores in making the transition out of the first year. For three weeks prior to the beginning of the fall semester, students participate in five intensive, faculty-led academic projects. Sophomore College students present their projects to the entire college and also participate in a series of faculty-led discussion groups. Professor Pat Jones, Chair of the Biological Sciences Department, values the opportunity to teach in the small-group settings offered by the Sophomore College (Manuel, 1996). This program began with significant support from the administration. Two of the original five faculty in the Sophomore College included Provost Condoleeza Rice and Vice Provost for Undergraduate Studies, Romon Saldivar, who also proposed the program.

Yale University (CT) established an informal advising evening for sophomores through each of its residential colleges in an attempt to address concerns about inadequate advising in the sophomore year (Schwebel, 1995). Unlike Yale first-year and upperclass students who already have advisors, Yale sophomores must

seek out their own advisors by the October advising time. Pierson College brings sophomores and seniors together during its sophomore evening to discuss topics including course distribution, foreign language requirements, majors, how to talk to a Department of Undergraduate Studies (DUS) professor, and fellowship and internship programs. In Ezra Stiles College, these sessions mix an informal reception offering light refreshments with presentations by the Master, Dean, Residential Fellows, and upperclass students. Sessions range in attendance from 60 to 100 sophomores. Krista Dove, Dean of Pierson College, notes that these informal advising sessions are not meant to take the place of the DUS or the faculty advisor, but they have, nonetheless, proved helpful for sophomores. Anecdotal evidence from faculty indicate that students who have participated in the sophomore evenings may be more knowledgeable about their major programs and more comfortable seeking advice from a variety of faculty members in their major departments.

Clemson University's (SC) Department of Marketing has also found it helpful to set aside evenings for sophomore advising. When the Admissions Department turned over recruitment of new students to the Department of Marketing, the number of marketing majors doubled in one year, from 400 to 800 (Mittelstaedt, 1999). Given that the marketing program does not place students in major classes until the spring of the sophomore year, this explosion of majors made the sophomore advising evenings a necessity. Also, for the first time the college appointed a dean responsible for advising. Although the radical increase in majors might be unique to Clemson, the lack of departmental connection among business majors is not. John Mittelstaedt, assistant professor in Clemson's Department of Marketing, notes that criteria for professional business associations dictate course requirements that place majors in general education courses for the first two years.

Without the sophomore advising evenings, and special departmental meetings designed for rapport building, most marketing majors would not have contact with major professors until their junior year (Mittelstaedt, 1999).

Some schools, such as *Wesleyan University* (CT), involve parents in the process of choosing a major. The Associate Dean of the College, Grissel Benitez Hodge, distributes a pamphlet, "Guide to Choosing and Declaring a Major," each fall to all sophomores. This process is also highlighted among the parents through *ParentLine*, an on-line journal for Wesleyan parents. A special issue, entitled "The Sophomore Slump or How to Choose a Major," explores the various dynamics of choosing a major from the parent and student perspectives. *The Pennsylvania State University* sophomore survey reveals a heavy reliance on parental input for major selections (Tomb, 1999).

Various schools address causes of dissatisfaction among sophomores, such as the sophomore meal plans at *Alma College* (MI) and *Tufts University* (MA), while others focus on efforts to better understand changes in majors among sophomores as a first step toward addressing the issues of the second year. *The University of North Carolina at Charlotte* uncovered the change of major issue in its Seven-Year Student Development Plan. During Phase 2 of the plan, an unexpected 20% of the sophomore pre-education students changed majors with no explanation (Hancock, 1998). Another study of 110 sophomore education majors revealed the high expectations of the first field experience. In turn, their perception of the program and the teaching vocation are heavily influenced by sophomore major and class assignments, such as these first field experiences (Rekkas, 1994).

California State University-Los Angeles (CSLA) determined that first-year transfer students were a seriously at-risk population. Nearly 30% of CSLA first-year transfer students have traditionally dropped out or been seriously at-risk during the sophomore year.

Acknowledging Tinto's (1987) assertion that half of the reasons for transfer attrition can be addressed by the institution, CSLA has required all transfer students to take a two-unit course to assist with adjustment to the new academic, intellectual, and social environment. The course's purpose is to help students deal with everyday concrete problems and issues. Faculty involved in researching transfer needs and developing the course are also producing a text on the subject, tentatively entitled *The Transfer Student's Guide to the College Experience* (Houghton Mifflin, 2000).[3]

One of the more innovative programs is found at *Ohio University* (1999) in Athens. The Sophomore Summer Program is offered during two, four-week sessions, beginning in mid-June and mid-July. Students completing their first year can choose to attend one or both of the sessions. Appended on the normal summer session class offerings, such as Accounting 101, this program offers dozens of free educational and recreational tours and seminars that give students in-depth knowledge of the services and opportunities of Ohio University. In other words, instead of just enrolling students in summer classes, this program provides intentional developmental and social outings. Approximately 20 educational activities are offered, ranging from library instruction and database search strategies, learning techniques, and time management to a "Tips Night" led by juniors and seniors. The program offers students the following opportunities:

- To concentrate on one or two tough classes
- To receive free one-on-one tutoring
- To live on campus or commute
- To reevaluate their majors with help
- To meet with faculty advisors and peer counselors
- To jump into dozens of free, fun recreational events
- To learn about many university services and programs and how to use them effectively

- To participate in educational and fun activities like stress management and relaxation

Addressing Developmental Concerns

In 1990, *Beloit College* discovered that a sophomore retreat proved popular among its returning students. At this retreat during orientation week, now in its 11th year, sessions on sophomore issues have been very well attended. Retreat sessions also include "Field and Career Services Programs," "World Affairs Center Programs," "Getting into Grad School," "Scholarships," and "Choosing a Major." This retreat is part of Beloit's "First-Year Initiatives/Sophomore Year Program." The two-year initiative has goals beyond student success which include fostering good working relationships between the academic and student development staffs and connecting both years through a seamless advising system. Each committee has a co-leader, one from the faculty and the other from student development. In addition to the sophomore retreat, sophomores participate in "Sophomore Sit-down Dinners" provided by Field and Career Services and the World Affairs Center. Presentations at these dinners address internships, field terms, and off-campus and overseas programs. An additional workshop on major decisions is provided for sophomores, along with a special sophomore course designed by the Chemistry and Biochemistry Department. Sophomores are tutored throughout their first two years on how to prepare a Comprehensive Academic Plan (CAP). A variety of informational leaflets are provided for both students and their parents. To expedite the preparation of the CAP and to help students make more intentional choices about their academic programs, students are required to complete a form that plans their next two years before beginning a study abroad program (Batterman & Ogurtsova, 1999).

Butler University (IN) has launched several initiatives with an eye toward sophomore success, which are treated in more detail in Chapter 1. Faculty liaison positions were created in order to assist students most likely to leave, according to profiles of at-risk students. The target group was students in the health sciences, such as, premedical, pre-dental, pre-physician assistants, and pre-pharmacy majors. The "transition faculty" helped to advise students into alternate health care options. Within one year, 50% fewer pre-health majors left the university.

One of the enduring traditions at *Azusa Pacific University* (CA), which is among the leaders in student development programs for small colleges, is its sophomore Walkabout Program. During orientation week each fall, more than 200 student leaders and numerous faculty and staff members head to the San Bernardino Mountains. Through ropes course initiatives, hikes, and other extreme challenges, personal fortitude and team-building concepts are experienced and applications to the tasks of the upcoming year are discussed. Most Walkabout members not only persist through their sophomore years to graduation, but they are among the most loyal alumni, joining Walkabout trips after graduation. The program has been replicated at *Greenville College* (IL), where it is known as the Links Program.

Cedar Crest College (PA) has an abbreviated form of Walkabout. Instead of a week, sophomores and staff members participate in a daylong complex adventure/treasure hunt involving activities to promote leadership, teamwork, creative problem-solving, questioning authority, and building community. Cedar Crest sees first-year student orientation as a time to explore self and others, while the sophomore year is a time to discover the group and a sense of commitment and belongingness. This connectivity is one of the issues that surfaced in Sylvia Hurtado's (1996) longitudinal study of first-year and sophomore Latino college students, implying a need for further college programming and monitoring in the sophomore year.

Saint Michael's College (VT) has established a Sophomore Development Office to focus on personal, social, and academic concerns in the second year, especially among academically at-risk students. The Sophomore Development Coordinator, Michael Ohler, stays in regular contact with sophomores and has launched numerous initiatives, such as the Emerging Leaders Program and The Personal Plan (which looks at career and life purpose).[4] The principles guiding this program are those that undergird sophomore programming at the *College of William and Mary* (VA), the *University of Texas*, and the *University of Nebraska*. The number of clients for Ohler's office has steadily increased, and the majority of probationary students gain full standing by the beginning of the second semester of the sophomore year. Ohler also surveys sophomores about satisfaction and has found the greatest dissatisfaction in the areas of student representation and course selection. Sophomores are most satisfied with student services and living situations. The latter response may correspond to changes in housing assignments for sophomores: First-year students live in a common area with 25 residents to every one resident advisor, while sophomores live on halls with a 50 to 1 ratio. The majority of written comments in his surveys note dissatisfaction about course selections and advising, a subject addressed by Anderson and Schreiner in Chapter 5. In 1997, Ohler noted, "Through discussion with other professionals it was determined that perhaps sophomores are trying to figure out who and how they want to be . . . Sophomore students go through a tremendous transition . . . [they] suffer from what I'll call the 'new baby in the house' syndrome [incoming first-year students]." The Student Development Office at Saint Michael's College has published his conclusion that there is indeed a sophomore slump and has produced a "Sophomore Slump [Inventory]" to help students identify and manage issues and concerns in the sophomore year (Figure 2).

Kalamazoo College (MI) requires its sophomores to engage in some type of practical career service during their second year. This experience helps them bring their potential career and academic discipline into

Figure 2
Sophomore Slump Inventory, Saint Michael's College

- What am I doing here at Saint Michael's College?
- What am I doing here at this program?
- Why do I have more questions now than when I first got here?
- Who are these people I hang around with that I thought were my friends?
- Why am I majoring in this, if I don't even like it?
- Why am I completely overwhelmed all the time?
- Why don't I have any time to relax?
- Why don't I have any idea what I'm gonna do when I grow up?
- Why don't my parents leave me alone about not knowing what I want to do when I grow up?
- How could I have acted like that last year?
- Why am I not having nearly as much fun as I did last year?
- Does everyone think I am weird?
- Why do I feel like I could cry if someone looks at me the wrong way?

If you have asked yourself 3 or more of the preceding questions since you arrived here this semester you could be suffering from a Sophomore Slump.

---

focus. Many students do not end up in this career, but the experience itself helps to raise issues about career choice and course application.

The University of Central Florida's LEAD Scholars Program transcends both the first and second years. This program has shown a remarkable success rate among its participants, compared to their non-LEAD colleagues. From 1995 to 1997, LEAD students persisted at a rate 16% greater than that of their contemporaries (University of Central Florida, 1999). Participants take one Foundations of Leadership course each semester for five semesters. These courses have both class and lab components and are designed to address 12 leadership competencies. The first year focuses on a successful beginning, and the sophomore year focuses on the choices typically made in the second year. The latter includes the following components: experiential leadership opportunities, LEAD classes, major/career exploration lab, serving as a mentor, leadership positions (e.g., LEAD Scholars Association), assistantships, externships, and practica. The assistantship program for sophomores is handled through an application process from the pool of successful first-year participants. These are paid positions and are intended to create mentoring relationships between faculty and administrators and LEAD scholars and to provide service and support for academic and administrative departments. The LEAD Scholars Association consists of seven teams that manage the various areas of interest in the LEAD Scholars Program. These teams are identified by team coordinators: technology coordinator, social coordinator, service coordinator, historian, editor of newsletter, speakers coordinator, and athletic coordinator. Among other events, these teams plan an on-campus Leadership Week, supported by various academic departments, to celebrate leadership. All LEAD scholars are required to complete a minimum of 10 service hours per semester. One option is to participate in an Alternative Spring Break. Recent spring break projects have provided assistance to seriously ill children at the Boggy Creek Gang Camp near Eustis, Florida and with building houses for low income families in Kentucky (University of Central Florida, 1999).[5]

The Sophomore Schmooze is among the various programs at the *University of Rochester* (NY) designed to facilitate sophomore success. The Sophomore Class Committee, which plans and implements sophomore-targeted educational and social programs and events, administers this program. Committee members represent various offices, including the Dean of Sophomores, Residence Life, Interdisciplinary/Special Programs, Student Activities, Career Center, Alumni Relations, Academic Support, and the English Department. In addition to the Schmooze, which brings sophomores together with the sophomore advising team, there are at least six other main events. The largest of these is the Sophomore Night with the President. Informational programs include the Sophomore Information table in the middle of campus, a Summer Jobshop, and a Study Abroad Fair. Other programming includes a Tour of Rochester (museum and recreational activities) and a Trip to Niagara Falls (during Fall Break). Students evaluate the program highly, with the most serious complaints coming from juniors and seniors who feel left out. The 1997 Recommendations for the Residential College Commission provides a helpful list of principles and key strategies for sophomore programming (Subcommittee on Sophomores, 1997). Dean Matt Hecker of *St. Olaf's College* (MN) would concur with these various options for sophomores. In his online "Ask the Dean" column, he encourages sophomores to liven up their college careers with a few new activities (Hecker 1994).

To this point, the examples of programming are addressed to the traditional, 18- to 22-year-old student. Lessons may also be drawn from programs for non-traditional students, especially in light of the fact that only 1.5 million of the nation's students are residential. For example, the average age of students in the 105 California community colleges—a significant cohort of students on the west coast—is 26 (Hallberg, 1999). One of the nation's largest and most successful non-traditional programs is housed at *Indiana Wesleyan University* (http://www.indwes.edu). An expansive cohort model in its adult programs places more than 7,000 students in cohort groups, perhaps one of the largest learning community models in the nation. During their second year of college, these students remain in the same cohort as their first year. For several consecutive years, the graduation rate for among participating students has been more than 80%. Rafael Heller (1998) asks, "Is there any evidence that these reforms work?" Citing examples at Holy Cross University, LaGuardia Community College, Daytona Beach Community College (FL), Western Michigan University and Temple University (PA), Heller finds "high levels of engagement and satisfaction" in the cohort approach (p. 11). IWU has found that it works to keep them in these groups beyond their first year.

Concluding Remarks

Educators from a variety of institutions of higher education are interested in addressing the needs of sophomores. Initial studies reveal that problems among sophomores are cause for concern and correlate with attrition. Also, these sophomore issues stretch beyond the academic arena. To this point, the preponderance of questions, suggestions, and programs address developmental issues more often than academic concerns. Hundreds of conference participants from a wide range of universities nationwide have identified categories of developmental issues among sophomores. Concomitantly, many existing sophomore programs address these issues. However, professionals who work with sophomores need resources. This monograph is one effort to synthesize a variety of approaches to help educators plan their own approaches and consider methods for attaining the necessary resources.

Notes

[1] Roberts Wesleyan University and Eastern College will be participating in a pilot study in Fall 2000. The seven schools participating in this study include Geneva, Asbury, Azusa Pacific, George Fox, Huntington, and Calvin. All schools submitted HERI reports in 1998.

[2] Corbin Smyth is the Director of Co-Curricular Programs at the University of Indianapolis. For more information, see the department's semester-by-semester handouts on The Lecture/Performance Series.

[3] Pattengale reviewed the prospectus for the office of Barbara Heinssen, Director of Student Success Programs and College Survival in December 1999.

[4] The author wishes to thank Michael Ohler from making his materials and correspondence available to us.

[5] In addition to reviewing the LEAD Scholars Program Student Handbook and Resource Manual, Pattengale was in correspondence with Jan Lloyd, Associate Director of the LEAD Scholars Program (1999-2000). For more information, visit the LEAD Scholars program website at http://pegasus.cc.usc.edu/~lsp.

References

ACT, Inc. (2000, February 16). *College dropout rate improves, but graduation rate falls.* [News Release]. Iowa City, IA: Author. Retrieved August 18, 2000 from the World Wide Web: http://www.act.org/news/releases/2000/02-16-00.html

Batterman, G., & Ogurtsova, O. (1999). *The Beloit College sophomore year program: A collaboration between faculty and student affairs.* Paper presented at the NACADA National Conference, Denver, CO.

Bence, C. (2000). *Survey of PHL 180: Becoming a world changer.* Marion, IN: Indiana Wesleyan University.

Blair, R. (1994, March). *The Westminster writing assessment program: A model for small colleges*. Paper presented at the 45th Annual Meeting of the Conference on College Composition and Communication, Nashville, TN.

Chickering, A. W. (1969). *Education and identity*. Jossey-Bass, San Francisco.

Davidson, B. S., & Muse, C. T. (1994). *A ten-year longitudinal study comparing 1980 freshman students' persistence to graduation at two selected universities*. (ERIC Document Reproduction Service No. ED 372 682)

Flanagan, W. (1990). *Sophomore retention: The missing strategy in small college retention efforts*. Unpublished dissertation. University of Wisconsin-Madison.

Flanagan, William (2000, March 1). Phone interview by J. Pattengale.

Hallberg, K. (1999, November 5). E-`mail correspondence from Hallberg to Roxanne Duvivier. Also, numerous correspondences to Pattengale, 1999.

Hancock, D. R. (1998). *The seven-year student development plan—A one-year retrospective*. Paper presented at the Annual Meeting of the Association of Teacher Educators Dallas, TX. (ERIC Document Reproduction Service No. ED 417 149)

Hecker, M. (1994, November 18). Ask the dean.108. *Campus Memo*. Northfield, MN: St. Olaf College. Retrieved November 18, 1994 from the World Wide Web: http://www.stolaf.edu/inside/

Heller, R. (1998, Fall). Learning communities: What does the research show? *Peer Review, 11*.

Houghton Mifflin, Co. (2000). *The transfer student's guide to the college experience*. [Book Prospectus]. Author: New York.

Hurtado, S., et al (1996). Latino student transition to college: assessing difficulties and factors in successful college adjustment. *Research in Higher Education, 37* (2), 135-57.

Johnson, D.S., & Hodges, R.B. (1990, april 8). Undergraduate students as facilitators in freshman classes. [Internal memorandum]. San Marcos, TX: College of General Studies, Southwest Texas State University.

Lemons. L. J., & Douglas, R. (1987). A developmental perspective on the sophomore slump. *NASPA Journal, 24*(3), 15-19.

Manuel, D. (1999, Nov/Dec). Sophomore success story: Seminars help second-year students battle 'slump'. *Stanford Today Online*. Retrieved August 28, 2000 from the World Wide Web: http://www.stanford.edu/dept/news/stanfordtoday/ed/9611/9611ncf101.shtml

Margolis, G. (1976). Unslumping our sophomores: Some critical observations and strategies. *Journal of the American College Health Association, 25*(2), 133-76.

Mittelstaedt, J. (1999, February 6). Book project. Email correspondence from Mittelstaedt to J. Pattengale.

Moore, B. (1998, March). Class of 2000 sophomores. *Penn State Pulse*. Retrieved August 28, 2000 from the World Wide Web: http://www.sa.psu.edu/sara/pulse/c2k98.shtml

Moore, B. (2000, March 2). Phone interview by J. Pattengale.

Noel, L., & Levitz, R. (1991). Beating the sophomore slump. *Recruitment and Retention in Higher Education, 5*(11), 1-3.

Ohio University. (1999). Summer program information. [On-line] Available at: http://www.ohiou.edu/summer

Ohler, M. (1997). *The concept of the

sophomore slump: A few thoughts and reflections on what I learned in my first semester. Letter from Ohler to his colleagues at Saint Michael's College (Student Life Office/Winooski Park, Colchester, Vermont 05439).

Rekkas, A. J. (1994, October 13). *Early field experience: How well are students' expectations met?* Paper presented at the Annual Meeting of the Midwestern Educational Research Association, Chicago, IL.

Richards, B. F., & Cariaga-Lo, L. (1994, September). Curriculum type and sophomore students' preparation time for the USMLE step 1 examination. *Evaluation and the Health Professions, 17*(3), 329-43.

Schwebel, S. (1995, September 16). Advising aims to prevent the dreaded sophomore slump. *Yale Daily News.* Retrieved August 28, 2000 from the World Wide Web: http:/www.yale.edu/ydn/paper/9.16/9.16.95storyno.CC.html

Smith, B. (in process). *Sophomore Retention: The common characteristics of academic and social integration of students in selected christian colleges.* Unpublished doctoral dissertation, State University of New York at Buffalo.

Smyth, C. (2000, January 28). Correspondence from Corbin Smyth to Stephanie Foote.

Spartanburg Methodist College (Fall, 1999). SMC 103 syllabus. Available from Spartanburg Methodist College, 1200 Textile Road, Spartanburg, SC 29301-0009.

Subcommittee on Sophomores. (1997). *Recommendations for the residential college commission.* Rochester, NY: University of Rochester. Retrieved August 28, 2000 from the World Wide Web: http://www.rochester.edu:80/student-srvcs/RCC/ARCHIVES/97/sophomor.htm

Tinto, Vincent (1987). *Leaving college.* Chicago: The University Press of Chicago.

Tomb, L. S. (1999, Winter). The sophomore slump or how to choose a major. *ParentLine, 11,*1-2. Wesleyan University. Retrieved from the World Wide Web: http://www.wesleyan.edu/parents/parentline.html

University of Central Florida (1999). *LEAD scholars program student handbook and resource manual: 1999-2000 academic year.* Orlando, FL: Author

Wilder, J. (1993, Spring). The sophomore slump: A complex developmental period that contributes to attrition. *College Student Affairs Journal, 12,* 18-27.

Curricular Issues For Sophomores

by Jerry G. Gaff

Chapter 4

Every time scholars focus on a particular kind of student, such as college sophomores, and seek ways to assure that those individuals receive an effective college education, the remedies recommended turn out to be good education—not just for the particular group identified but for all students.

The first time I discovered this phenomenon was in the late 1960s when I was a young researcher at the Center for Research and Development in Higher Education at the University of California, Berkeley. A group of colleagues, led by Paul Heist (1968), were studying "creativity" in college students. They found that creative students did not do well within the strictures of the usual curricular structure. Their evidence indicated that these students do better in alternative curricula, with greater opportunities to pursue their own interests, more individual attention from professors, and a community of peers with intellectual and creative interests who both supported and challenged them. My thought at the time was, "Of course! Who wouldn't?"

Later, interest turned to other kinds of students and special educational programs designed for them: talented students and honors programs, at-risk students and programs of support (Erickson & Strommer, 1991), adult students and adult programs, women students and women's studies programs (Musil, 1992), and minority students and special programs for them (Smith & Associates, 1997). In each case, the focus on the needs of particular kinds of students generated ideas that turned out to constitute good education for other students.

And now comes along a volume devoted to college sophomores, another special group of students, and we are asked to think about how colleges can best promote their education and development. This is an important question, because, if my observation is correct, it will allow us to once again discover what constitutes good education for sophomores—and for other college students.

The Curricular Problem

Some of the problems faced by first-year and sophomore students can be traced to the fact that they are completing general education requirements, and most are not yet deeply involved in their majors. Virtually all general education programs utilize some kind of distributed study, and the introductory survey is a common course structure. The value of the content of most required general education courses is not immediately apparent to students, and typically the purposes, rationale, and utility of the learning are not well explained. Students seldom have any kind of special relationship with a faculty member teaching an introductory course, and student peer groups around Psych 101 or General Chemistry, for example, are not often formed. Such a structure tends to create, in the words of a curriculum review committee at Hamilton College, a "curricular dead space" that leaves students "free-floating." In a survey course, it takes an unusual course and instructor to engage students intellectually and emotionally.

Some years ago, I directed the Project on General Education Models (GEM) and invited institutions to apply to participate in a collaborative effort to improve the core curriculum. As part of the application, applicants were instructed to state what was wrong with their general education program and what they wanted to improve. Virtually all—research universities, comprehensive institutions, liberal arts colleges, and community colleges—employed a loose distribution system in which students were required to take two courses from column A, three from column B, etc. I analyzed the

problems the writers of the proposals attributed to this curricular arrangement, and five common characteristics of the general education model became apparent.

1. The requirements lack a rationale and are not based on a considered educational analysis of a philosophy of what is an "educated person." They are more often the result of a political compromise among the faculty in different departments.
2. The programs are fragmented; they lack coherence; and connections between courses are seldom made or expected.
3. Lacking a rationale and coherence, students see these requirements largely as hoops to jump through. Advised by their faculty members to "get their general education requirements out of the way," students seek to do precisely that.
4. Senior faculty flee from teaching "service courses" and leave these responsibilities to junior faculty, adjuncts, or teaching assistants, signaling to students that they are not as important as courses in their majors.
5. No single person is responsible for administering the distribution requirements, and no single body is responsible for assuring that the program is rigorous, engaging, and useful to students.

What does it mean for a sophomore student not to understand why he or she is taking courses that for some reasons, mysterious to them, are required, but not valued by the senior faculty and not connected to each other or to their major? What does it mean to be a student when one is not connected in any meaningful academic way with other students or faculty in required distributional courses?

In these circumstances, academic study becomes, to a great extent, a solitary pursuit and more a matter of compliance than of commitment. Relationships with other students, if any, tend to be based not primarily on academic concerns but on social ties of some sort. This condition is a good definition of an "at-risk" student, and this common curricular pattern increases whatever risks students bring with them to college.

First-year programs are a creative response to this condition. They seek to create bonds between new students, connect each student to a professor or staff member who teaches a first-year course, and provide information about how to survive in college. The sophomore students, though facing the same basic set of conditions, typically have no curricular structure helping them to grow educationally or personally.

Indeed, the condition facing sophomore students is largely the same one facing first-year students, except that they are (at least) a year older, have more experience navigating the institution, and may have made some friends. But sophomores, if they had benefited from one of the many first-year programs, may experience a loss of this academic community and feel even more alone than if they had not realized that academic community could exist.

I should hasten to add that distributional study does not need to have the atomized and fragmented qualities that very often characterize it. At the very least, the rationale behind the curriculum and the purposes of the courses can be explained to students, who might begin to see the larger world available to educated people. And as leaders of learning communities realize, required courses can be linked, such as a writing course with a course in a discipline, so that students write about the topics in the disciplinary course. They also can be clustered around a theme or issue of concern to students. Such courses, which are explicitly parts of learning communities, are more powerful contexts for learning all sorts of content than the more common stand-alone courses. The problem is that too often these steps are not actually taken, and students tend to drift through a curriculum that is less than it might be. What is to be done?

Curricular Practices to Engage Sophomore Students

Several institutions have developed curricular structures and practices that engage sophomore students and seek to correct the conditions cited above, although the attention given to sophomores is usually far less than that given to first-year students. Below are several examples of curricular practices that can address the "curricular dead space" of sophomores. This list is suggestive and not meant to be exhaustive. Indeed, few institutions do anything specifically designed for sophomores, and the opportunities to improve their conditions of learning are many.

Core Curriculum

A true core curriculum that extends through all four years is operated by a small number of institutions as diverse as *St. Joseph's College* (small, private, and Catholic) and *Brooklyn College, City University of New York* (large, public, and non-sectarian). In such a curriculum, second-year students have specific curriculum components presented to them, complete with a well-articulated rationale and an opportunity to become invested in it.

Learning Communities

Some institutions operate intentional learning communities that allow groups of students to focus on issues and themes cutting across disciplines and connecting content in different courses. *Portland State University* (OR), for example, requires first-year students to participate in a year-long thematic learning community called Inquiry in which they learn to ask meaningful questions and conduct college-level inquiry. A smaller learning community is expected of second-year students. This assures that each student in this large commuter institution continues to be placed within a serious and vital academic community. A growing body of research documents that students in such academic communities, as a group, learn more, are more satisfied, and are more likely to remain enrolled than those without such communities (Matthews, Smith, MacGregor, & Gabelnick, 1996).

Some institutions place a learning community within a residence hall. Such is the case of the Bradley Learning Community at the *University of Wisconsin, Madison*, a first-year and sophomore year program of study focusing on the environment. This arrangement gives all students in the group a common set of concerns and a common language that provides opportunities for them to continue the classroom discussions within the residence hall.

Specialized Courses

Sophomore interdisciplinary seminar. *Hamilton College* (NY) requires a common sophomore interdisciplinary seminar that includes a public presentation; it is part of four required interdisciplinary courses in the first and second college years. The faculty hope that it will do for general education what the senior project does for the major: provide an end point for a sequence of courses and demonstrate the knowledge and skills students have developed.

Reflective seminars. Students typically do their studies, complete their courses, and continue taking courses until they graduate without a structured opportunity to reflect on their learning. A few colleges have instituted a reflective seminar for students to reflect on their learning, analyze how well their course of study is progressing, and examine what it adds up to. *Olivet* (MI) and *Wagner* (NY) *Colleges* are examples that formally involve sophomores in this kind of activity.

Portfolio Development

Franklin Pierce College (NH) not only expects students to reflect on their learning, but it assists students in assessing how well they are doing in relation to the learning goals that guide the curriculum. Annually students assemble materials that bear on their achievement of the specific goals adopted by the faculty and progressively document their achievement of the educational goals. *Alverno College* (WI) has pioneered the assessment of specified educational goals and integrates such assessment into the educational process itself.

Sophomore Workshops

A survey of students conducted by the office of the Dean of the College at *Princeton University* (NJ) revealed that they would welcome the kind of academic attention that had been directed at first-year students. Leaders piloted a series of Sophomore Workshops, non-credit, voluntary, mini-courses that gave opportunities to work closely with faculty members. A range of topics was included, such as the physics of blood plasma, understanding autism, the linguistics of science fiction, and the tango. Each workshop typically met three or four evenings and culminated in some special event, such as a field trip or attendance at an artistic performance. Although the director of the program credited it with reinvigorating the intellectual life of the residences, faculty involvement dropped so low that other strategies are currently being considered.

Educational Experiences Beyond the Classroom

Elon College (NC) encourages its students to participate in five kinds of educational experiences beyond the classroom: research, internships, study abroad, service, and leadership for some activity or organization. The college provides students with a co-curriculum transcript that documents the activities completed by students, some of them while they are sophomores.

Service learning. Like Elon, many institutions encourage or require service learning, but *St. Francis College* (PA) requires 10 hours of service learning as an integral part of its Introduction to Religion course, which is usually taken in the sophomore year. Drawing on its Franciscan mission, the college expects all students to engage in service in the schools, public agencies, and churches, and this requirement has provided powerful new experiences for students. It has also injected new dynamism into the first course of the religion sequence, making the entire sequence more meaningful.

Dinner discussions. Davidson College (NC) completed a series of dinner discussions with second-year students. Individuals were invited in random groups to have dinner with a faculty or staff member. Although most expressed satisfaction with their experience, large numbers wanted more contact with faculty members. Few had developed a close relationship with a faculty member, despite the fact that all had expected they would do so at Davidson.

This brief excursion illustrates that a rich variety of educational activities can be engaging to sophomore students and can help them overcome a sense of floating freely through a poorly understood curriculum, of academic isolation, and of a disconnect between their personal aspirations and their academic requirements. How much more could academics do if they were more intentional about the particular problems faced by sophomores and more attentive to finding solutions to those problems?

Principles for Curricular Practice

Research has documented that several principles are valuable guides to the development of the curriculum and the provision of certain kinds of learning experiences. The above practices partake of one or more of these principles.

1. *Involvement in learning.* Astin (1993) not only articulated a theory that academic involvement promotes student cognitive and affective development, but he has also

documented its empirical effects. He concludes, "Learning, academic performance, and retention are positively associated with academic involvement, involvement with faculty, and involvement with student peer groups" (p. 394). On the other hand, he reports:

A wide spectrum of cognitive and affective outcomes is negatively affected by forms of involvement that either isolate the student from peers or remove the student physically from the campus: living at home, commuting, being employed off campus, being employed full-time, and watching television. (p. 395)

Therefore, any curricular practice that increases academic involvement and decreases the factors that undermine that involvement should enhance the education of sophomore students, as well as others.

2. *Integration into the community.* Tinto (1987), analyzing the conditions under which students leave college, developed a theory of social integration. Examining a great deal of empirical research, he concluded that "...the success not only of retention programs, but of education programs generally, hinges on the construction of educational communities at the college, program, and classroom level which integrate students into the on-going social and intellectual life of the institution" (p. 188). According to this analysis, curricular practices that connect students to one another and to faculty members and engage them in serious intellectual inquiry—whether through a first-year course on the nature of inquiry, undergraduate research, or participation in a learning community—will enhance the education of students.

3. *Connected learning.* Cross (1999) draws from learning theory to assert that learning is about making connections:

Cognitive and neural connections are made through establishing and keeping in good repair the [brain] pathways that connect new learning to existing knowledge. Social connections are utilized to challenge thought and to engage students actively in questioning and thinking about knowledge that is rooted in the culture and language of our society. Experiential connections are necessary to assure that students conduct an active lifelong conversation between experience and learning. (p. 23)

The implication of this formulation is that curricular practices that connect students' ideas across courses and fields, connect ideas with one's personal life, and connect ideas with social and cultural issues are powerful educational devices. This helps to explain the significance of many forms of experiential learning, of learning communities, and of strategies for students to reflect periodically on the learning they are achieving.

Conclusion

Sophomore students, often invisible to curriculum planners, ought to have a claim on their attention. They face a number of the same kinds of problems faced by first-year students, but they do not have the benefit of the specially designed first-year programs. Yet, some colleges and universities are taking a number of curricular steps that constitute good education for this group of students. Three different but related theoretical positions suggest directions for enhancing the curriculum for sophomores, as well as other students. As Tinto writes, "The essential character of such [educationally powerful] communities lies not in the formal structures they construct, but in the underlying values which inspire their construction" (p. 181). For institutions to develop curricula that are friendly to sophomores, they will have to commit to help all the students they admit to succeed—and then create involving curricula that integrate them into the academic community and help them to forge meaningful connections. That is a tall order but one that is eminently achievable.

References

Astin, A. W. (1993). *What matters in college*. San Francisco: Jossey-Bass.

Cross, K. P. (1999). *Learning is about making connections*. The Cross Papers Number 3. Mission Viejo, CA: League for Innovation.

Erickson, B. L, & Strommer, D. W. (1991). *Teaching college freshmen*. San Francisco: Jossey-Bass.

Heist, P. A. (Ed.). (1968). *The creative college student*. San Francisco: Jossey-Bass.

Matthews, R. S., Smith, B. L., MacGregor, J., & Gabelnick, F. (1996). Creating learning communities. In J. G. Gaff and J. L. Radcliff (Eds.), *Handbook of the undergraduate curriculum* (pp. 457-475). San Francisco: Jossey-Bass.

Musil, K. M. (1992). *The courage to question: Women's studies and student learning*. Washington, DC: Association of American Colleges and National Women's Studies Association.

Smith, D. G. & Associates. (1997). *Diversity works*. Washington, DC: Association of American Colleges and Universities.

Tinto, V. (1987) *Leaving college*. Chicago: University of Chicago Press.

• • •

For more information about
the programs cited in the text:

Core curriculum:

Rev. Timothy McFarland, C.PP.S., Coordinator of the Core Curriculum, St. Joseph's College, Rensselaer, Indiana

Ellen Belton, Dean of Undergraduate Studies, Brooklyn College, City University of New York

Learning Communities:

Charles White, Associate Dean, College of Liberal Arts and Sciences, Portland State University, Portland, Oregon

Learning Communities in Residence Halls Cal Bergman, Residence Life Complex Coordinator, Bradley Learning Community, University of Wisconsin, Madison

Thomas Klein, Director of the Chapman Learning Center, Bowling Green State University Bowling Green, Ohio

Sophomore Common Interdisciplinary Seminar:

Bobby Fong, Dean of the Faculty, Hamilton College, Clinton, New York

Reflective Seminars:

Donald L. Tuski, Associate Vice President for Academic Affairs, Olivet College, Olivet, Michigan

Richard Guarasci, Provost, Wagner College, Staten Island, New York

Portfolio Development:

Kathleen O'Brien, Academic Dean, Alverno College, Milwaukee, Wisconsin

Gary Rook, Director of General Education, Franklin Pierce College, Rindge, New Hampshire

Service Learning:

Kathleen Owens, Vice President for Academic Affairs, St. Francis College, Loretto, Pennsylvania

Sophomore Workshops:

Hank Dobin, Associate Dean of the College, Princeton University

Educational Experiences Beyond the Classroom:

Jerry Francis, Provost, Elon College, Elon College, North Carolina

Dinner Discussions:

Scott Denham, Associate Professor of German, Davidson College, Davidson, North Carolina

Advising for Sophomore Success

by Edward "Chip" Anderson and Laurie A. Schreiner

Chapter 5

The academic advising relationship holds particular promise as a strategy for supporting sophomores and encouraging their success—especially within the context of broader sophomore year programming. If, as earlier chapters have suggested, it is crucial for the institution to continue the good work of first-year programming, advising is a structure that already exists and that can be used to greater advantage with sophomores.

The advising picture for sophomores, however, is sometimes rather bleak. Too often, sophomores who have yet to declare a major are assigned to advisors at random, and many are sent to those advisors who have the least number of advisees—not always a good sign of the advisor's expertise. Even sophomores who have declared a major and are assigned an advisor in their major department do not always receive the kind of developmental advising needed at this stage in their educational careers. As a result, many sophomores find the advising relationship to be less than satisfying (Juillerat, 2000), and often a far cry from the special advising they received as first-year students. Advising in the sophomore year needs to pick up where the first-year advising left off—with a continued emphasis on planning and goal-setting.

This planning and goal-setting element of advising, begun in the first year, is particularly important to continue in the sophomore year. Frequently, first-year students are too distracted by the demands of a new environment to process all the attempts to plan and set goals (Lemons & Richmond, 1987). Sophomores are a little more settled and are ready for a more complete plan that will give them a sense of direction for the next three years. Yet, this need for a plan comes at a time when pressures to perform academically are mounting, when the need to make a decision about their major is looming ominously, and when the support and attention of the institution is often at its lowest (Juillerat, 2000).

At this point in a student's career, an advising relationship with a caring faculty member can make all the difference. We know from previous research that faculty-student contact is a vital ingredient in student success and persistence (Astin, 1993). The advising relationship is the natural structure in which that contact can occur, and when the relationship focuses on developmental issues, planning, and goal setting, there is tremendous potential to impact sophomores' success and persistence.

In this chapter, we will explore two issues: (a) the concerns particular to sophomores that need to be addressed in the advising process and (b) how to design an advising program for sophomores. In this second area, we do not suggest particular structures—those need to be individually developed to fit each campus—but we do provide an outline of the tasks of sophomore advisors. By outlining their needs and issues and by recommending specific tasks or strategies to address these concerns, we hope to make the sophomore advising process more effective. In terms of structure, whether an institution has a sophomore advising center, special faculty who advise only undeclared sophomores, professional advisors who target sophomores, or a training program designed to highlight sophomores' issues and needs may not matter. The point is that sophomores do need a different kind of advising than they needed as first-year students. The remainder of this chapter is devoted to describing what that advising might look like.

Issues To Address in the Sophomore Advising Process

An advisor needs to be aware of four major issues when working with sophomores: (a)

dealing with an intensified curriculum, (b) career issues, (c) lack of academic and social integration, and (d) reduced motivation.

Dealing with an Intensified Curriculum

Sophomores are often in the "academic twilight zone." For those who have declared a major, the sophomore year is frequently designed as a weeding-out process, with myriad demanding pre-requisite courses set as hurdles to full acceptance in the major. Simultaneously, not fully into the "meat" of their major, sophomores are often completing general education requirements, many of which are the more difficult courses they avoided in their first year. Without the coherence often provided by institutional programming in the first year, sophomores may find themselves wondering why they are taking many of these courses. Focus group interviews we have conducted with sophomores reveal that often students simply are not looking forward to the year academically. As one sophomore said, "I came back eager to see friends and faculty I had missed all summer, but took one look at my schedule of classes and immediately felt depressed. There was not a single class I was looking forward to" (Schreiner, 1999). Being at the bottom of the heap in registration priorities only exacerbates the problem. Often sophomores have little choice as to the general education requirements that will complete their schedule and are closed out of many major courses as well—even if they *had* met the pre-requisites.

When sophomores look at their class schedules, too few of them see a coherent picture that will spur them on to their goal. They may find it difficult to have a sense of the "big picture" or where all the requirements are taking them. For students who have not declared a major, the lack of coherence can seem even greater. The advising process can provide students with the big picture. It can be akin to "showing students the box" as they are putting together the "jigsaw puzzle" of their curriculum (Cross, 1999). Working with an advisor, a sophomore can discover how the pieces fit and what pieces are needed in the coming year.

Major and Career Issues

A second advising issue for sophomores is that of declaring a major and selecting a career. Career issues can affect sophomores in different ways. Some sophomores have never given much thought to the career planning process throughout their first year and are now feeling pressured from all sides to declare a major and decide upon a career goal. Pressure from parents, friends, the institution, and even that which is self-imposed all combine to create a sense of urgency within the sophomore student. They know time is running out, that further delay will mean additional time and cost to graduate. But too few sophomores are even aware of the services a career center can provide. Once again, the advisor can help by explaining the services offered on campus and referring the student to the career center for the help needed.

Other sophomores have perhaps initially decided on a major and/or career, but are facing the harsh reality of their own limitations. Many advisors have encountered the student who has his or her heart set on being a physician but cannot pass general biology. Career issues for students who entered college with high hopes of a certain career and have had those hopes dashed are different from the career issues of students who have put little thought into the matter. And an advisor's role in each case will be different. Helping the student create "Plan B" is an important advising task for the sophomore year. The transition advisors at Butler University, referred to in Chapter 1 of this monograph, are a good example of a strategy for providing Plan B advising.

Unfortunately, many students fail to realize that one of the functions of college is career exploration. Instead, they think that if they have not decided on a major and career goal by the end of their sophomore year, they should not remain in college. In focus groups we have conducted, one of the most common statements we heard from sophomores was "I can't justify spending this amount of tuition when I don't know what I'm doing with my life" (Schreiner, 1999). These students seem to believe that a year or two working for minimum wage will offer them some kind of enlightenment on the perfect career. But what better place to explore career interests and options than in college, where role models abound and an advisor and career counselor are both available to provide individualized assistance? The role of the advisor in this instance is not only to refer students to the career center but also to help students see that being in college allows them to explore their career interests more fully. In addition, the advisor can assist students in identifying their strengths and matching those strengths to particular kinds of work environments. The advisor also can help students see how taking a variety of courses can prepare them for almost any major, without delaying graduation in the process. Again, many students mistakenly believe that particular academic majors lead to specific careers, not realizing that very few careers require a major in that field (elementary school teaching being a notable exception). Good advisors can help sophomores see the value of their education as providing a foundation and framework for a wealth of career opportunities.

Because of the importance of a broad education, advising should not become overly focused on career issues, however. Certainly sophomores need assistance in this area, but sophomores' advising needs go far beyond curricular and career issues.

Lack of Integration

At the root of curricular and career issues are two other issues: the lack of academic and social integration and the reduced motivation that accompanies it. Tinto (1987) theorizes that students enter college with varying characteristics and abilities that are continually modified by interactions with the academic and social systems of a college or university. Positive and successful interactions facilitate the integration of the student into the fabric of the institution, resulting in a greater commitment to the institution and ultimately resulting in persistence.

First-year experience programs are primarily aimed at fostering students' academic and social integration. And our institutional programming reflects that the integration process should be complete by the end of the first year. Yet for many sophomores the integration process may not be finished. Academically, they may be performing below their desired level. They may not have developed meaningful relationships with faculty and academic staff by the second year. For many reasons, they may not be fully engaged in the learning process. Socially, they may not be involved on campus or may not find it easy to become involved. They may not have found their "niche" on campus and may not feel as though they belong. They also may not have developed meaningful relationships with their peers. Again, we too often assume that these tasks will be completed by the end of the first year—especially if we have highly effective FYE programs! But not all sophomores have successfully met these demands as first-year students, and they may need another year to do so (Lemons & Richmond, 1987). The advisor can be a major ally in this process. In the advising relationship, students can develop a meaningful relationship with a faculty member and can discuss their academic progress along with any factors that may be interfering with their ability to meet their desired level of success. The advisor can also help the student understand how the "system" works and what it takes to navigate it successfully. The advisor can be a catalyst in the integration process, which is just as crucial for sophomores as it is for first-year students.

Reduced Motivation

The final, but perhaps most important, issue sophomore advising needs to address is the motivational "slump" that too often occurs in the sophomore year. This reduced motivation has a number of potential sources. Baker, McNeil, and Siryk (1985) postulate that a "matriculant myth" operates in the minds of many entering students, influencing their attitudes toward college. At the beginning of their college careers, this myth operates to create high and unrealistic expectations of what college will be like. Students learn from parents and family that these will be "the best years of their lives" (not realizing how selective their parents' memories are after more than 20 years!). They see romanticized portrayals of college life in the media and expect their own experience to match. They are then disillusioned when the reality does not match their expectation.

Not all students experience the effects of the matriculant myth, however. The myth is most pronounced in its effects when students are less familiar with the college they enter, do not participate much in campus activities or attain campus leadership positions, perform poorly in classes, or change majors frequently. A pronounced "myth effect" is also correlated with a higher incidence of leaving college before graduation (Baker, McNeil, & Siryk, 1985).

Knowing that poor academic performance, changing majors, and a lack of campus involvement are associated with greater disenchantment with college, the academic advisor can be in a position to intervene with "at-risk" students. This intervention ought to begin in the first year but should continue throughout the sophomore year. Encouraging students to become more involved on campus may help prevent some of the disenchantment. Helping students identify their strengths and teaching them how to capitalize on those strengths and how to match them to potential life goals and a major can also mediate the effects of the matriculant myth. As Baker, et al. (1985) note, "it would seem desirable to attempt interventions . . . aimed at improving awareness and understanding of self" (p. 101). They also suggest that the more realistic the student is about his/her abilities and performance in new environments, the less impact the myth has. So helping students form realistic expectations of college and of themselves may need to happen within the advising relationship, if that process has not occurred during the first year.

Reduced motivation can also stem from a "lack of aliveness" (Anderson & McGuire, 1996). For some sophomores, nothing has aroused their curiosity or engaged and stimulated their intellect or their passion. A lack of intellectual engagement leads naturally to reduced motivation. An academic advisor can work with students to uncover their passions and interests, guiding them to courses that have the potential to spark their intellectual curiosity.

For some sophomores, the reduced motivation may be due to fear that they do not have what it takes to succeed in college or that they have not made the right choice in coming to college. Not putting much effort into classes can save face—after all, failing when one "hasn't really tried" is not nearly as painful as failing after exerting one's full efforts. A lack of self-efficacy may accompany this fear. The fear may be based in the belief that they are not capable of succeeding in college. As Bandura (1982) notes, people lacking in self-efficacy often have not had the kind of experiences and support necessary to believe that they can succeed. As a result, they perceive themselves to be less competent than others; believing that they will not succeed, they do not approach opportunities with confidence. They either avoid any situation in which they believe they cannot be successful, or they give up early into the situation. From previous research done with first-year students, we know that persistence is a key factor in student success.

Those students who persist when things become difficult are the ones most likely to get higher grades and graduate from college; in fact, a "persistent spirit" accounts for 65% of the variation in students' GPA at the end of their first year of college (Schreiner, 1996).

As long noted in the field of organizational psychology (Herzberg, 1987), a key difference exists between what satisfies and motivates people and those factors which serve simply to prevent dissatisfaction. Herzberg's "motivation-maintenance theory" points out that satisfaction is produced by the presence of motivating factors. In the work world, these factors may be opportunities for personal growth, professional challenge, promotion opportunities, or degree of responsibility. For the student, motivating factors also may include opportunities for personal growth, academic challenge, increasing responsibility, opportunities for achievement and recognition, and being able to work with material that is interesting to them. Enhancing student motivation means we must find ways of engaging and challenging students, giving them increased responsibility and opportunities to achieve.

More recent research in this field (Locke & Latham, 1990; Lawler, 1991) adds to Herzberg's theory the importance of meaningful goals and the expectation that effort will result in a meaningful outcome. Lawler, for example, points out that the attractiveness of the outcomes, along with the ability to meet expectations, are what motivate a person to perform. For students, this may mean helping them discover the joy of learning, helping them see that education has many attractive outcomes beyond a specific career, and matching their strengths and abilities to appropriate courses and opportunities.

Often students are all too aware of their weaknesses but are not as aware of their strengths. Finding themselves in courses which highlight their weaknesses, or in courses which fail to spark their interest, can easily lead to reduced motivation (Anderson, 1997). Operating solely in one's area of weakness does little to energize any of us. And yet a quick glance at most FYE textbooks reveals an emphasis on assessing the student's ability to meet the challenges of college, with the assessment tools invariably producing "deficit scores"—scores that highlight an area in need of improvement.

How do we begin to discover strengths? Advisors can point out to students that indicators of strengths include (a) rapid learning; (b) a deep sense of satisfaction about an achievement; (c) hopes, dreams, and longings; (d) performance at levels of excellence, even if only for a short time; (e) experiencing a sense of destiny or "rightness;" (f) doing something well and seemingly effortlessly; (g) instant insights and understandings; (h) consistent patterns of success in a particular role, context, or set of tasks; (i) being passionate about something; and (j) experiencing joy and delight when engaged in an activity (Anderson, 1995).

Designing an Advising Program for Sophomores

In order to address the advising needs of sophomores, which we have outlined above, three key principles are integral to success. Rather than outline a particular model of advising, we prefer to outline these principles as foundational to any model.

Prevention

The best way to address sophomore needs is to provide students with the resources they need before they need them. Prevention is always easier than crisis intervention. Methods of preventing some of the common problems sophomores encounter include the following:

1. Suggest that first-year students not postpone all the difficult or less desirable courses until the sophomore year. Instead, they should use the first year to prepare for the sophomore year.

2. Conduct an orientation for sophomores. Communicate realistic expectations about the upcoming year, introduce students to their majors, connect them to faculty in their majors, and help them get to know upper-level students. Encourage their involvement in leadership opportunities on campus early in the semester.

3. Design courses for sophomores that are academically legitimate and yet address their experiences. Such courses might include Career Planning, Strengths-Based Learning, Learned Optimism and Learned Helplessness, Community Psychology, Positive Psychology, Attributional Processes, The Graduate School Experience, Motivation and Learning, and Inquiry—all of these are courses currently offered by institutions.

4. At the end of the first year, if the student is changing advisors, have the first-year advisor introduce the student to his/her next advisor. The new advisor could then conduct an "end-of-the-year" inventory or interview to discuss such questions as:

   1. How are you different from a year ago?

   2. What impact has college had on you so far?

   3. What had you hoped college would be like? What was it really like?

   4. What are your goals for your sophomore year? Imagine it's one year from now. What do you want to have happened by then?

5. What have been your greatest disappointments since you've been here? How have you coped? What strengths have helped you through the difficult times?

6. What would have to happen—and what would you need to do—to be able to say next year, "this has been a really good year"?

7. How well do you think you are fitting in here? Tell me about your roommate, your friends, the activities you are involved in on campus, and how you feel about your classes. How well do you think you will fit in as a sophomore here?

8. Have you discovered a system of learning, studying, or achieving goals that works best for you? What really helps you succeed academically? What have been your favorite classes? What academic experiences have been the most stimulating or influential so far?

9. What, if anything, would need to change for you to feel this is the right place for you to be?

This process of "taking stock" at the end of the first year, whether done with the first-year advisor or with the new advisor, can help students think about their experiences, reflect on their strengths, and prepare themselves for the sophomore year.

Another strategy for the end of the first year is to intentionally ask first-year students to make commitments for the sophomore year. For example, three key areas in which prospective sophomores could be asked to make commitments include:

1. *A commitment to the next class of first-year students*. Asking them to be peer leaders in the first-year seminar, or during orientation, can give prospective

sophomores not only something to which they can look forward but also a sense of being needed and making an important contribution to the incoming class.

2. *A commitment to a specific and focused area of learning*. Perhaps the student is not yet ready to declare a major, or is facing a year of difficult courses that are less than engaging. By asking students to commit to a specific area of learning, we are encouraging students to become engaged in the learning process and to take ownership for it. As psychologist Claude Steele (1997) notes, courses and programs that challenge and stretch students beyond their current level of ability have the potential to activate within students a desire to achieve that is rarely present in courses which seek to remediate. Asking prospective sophomores to commit to an area of learning that capitalizes on their strengths and promises to challenge and engage them holds particular promise for preventing the reduced motivation so often seen in the sophomore year.

3. *A commitment to service*. Elsewhere in this monograph, Jerry Gaff points out the effectiveness of service-learning programs in meeting sophomores' needs. By asking prospective sophomores to commit to service, we are increasing the potential for their learning experiences to engage their whole person. In addition, by focusing beyond themselves, sophomores can derive meaning and purpose in a year which may have otherwise been only endured as a necessary step to graduation.

Planning

The second principle, which is integral to an effective advising program for sophomores, is planning. Because one of the most common complaints we have heard from sophomores in focus groups is that it is difficult for them to justify paying tuition when they do not know what they are doing with their lives, it would seem that an advising relationship that helps the student identify his/her strengths and develop a plan for capitalizing on those strengths as they explore their options and select a major, would be a major benefit to sophomores. Examples of types of planning that would benefit sophomores include the following:

1. *Focusing on the career planning process.* Students do not know the process involved in choosing a career. Explain the process to students and teach them decision-making and goal-setting skills.

2. *Helping students develop "Plan B" in case their original plan for a major or career falls through.* Ask them to think through what would be their second choice if they were not able to succeed in their first choice of a major. Figures 1 and 2 represent the elements of good course selection and demonstrate the relationship between course, major, and career selection. By using visuals such as these, students can begin to picture the planning process and how all the elements relate to one another.

3. *Helping students develop a sense of the big picture by helping them develop a four-year plan.* Map out the course requirements for their chosen major; help them see where the core courses, a minor, and electives fit in.

4. *Working with the financial aid office to include financial planning in the students' planning process.* Particularly for those institutions which have a "one-stop shopping,"— advising center with financial aid resources in the same area—this process helps students see their commitment to college as a long-term investment with steps to take along the way to graduate successfully. The current system of advising, registration, and billing which is in place in many institutions encourages students to make a decision about re-

investing in college each semester or, at best, each year.

Participation

To address sophomores' needs for involvement and engagement in learning in and out of the classroom, an effective advising relationship will foster students' participation in the life of the college in the following ways:

On-campus involvement. Encourage sophomores to be peer leaders in new student orientation or the first-year course. Provide a leadership practica for interested sophomores. Encourage students to seek out leadership opportunities on campus.

Involvement in the major. Encourage students to volunteer in a setting related to their major, to gain work experience and also to gain a sense of whether this is the right major for them. Invite them to attend departmental activities in the major that interests them. Introduce them to the value of service-learning courses or experiences, or to experiential education.

Involvement with faculty. Help students see the value of seeking out faculty and, if possible, working with faculty on a research project. Introduce sophomores to the mentoring programs that may exist on campus, or help them select a potential mentor. Point out that it would benefit them to take at least one class that is small in size or directly related to their interests or major area, to give them an opportunity to become better acquainted with faculty.

By carefully crafting sophomore advising experiences to focus on prevention, planning, and participation, we can begin to address the reduced motivation, performance, and persistence that is found in too many of our sophomores. With intentionality and effort, the notorious "sophomore slump" can become "sophomore success."

Figure 1

Elements of Good Course Selection (Anderson, 1998)

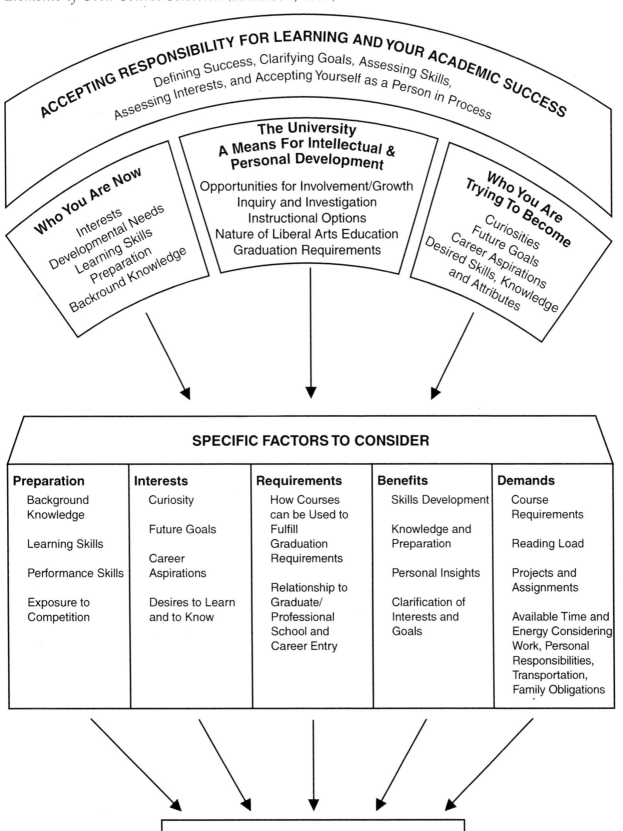

Figure 2

Relating Course, Major, And Career Selection (Anderson, 1988)

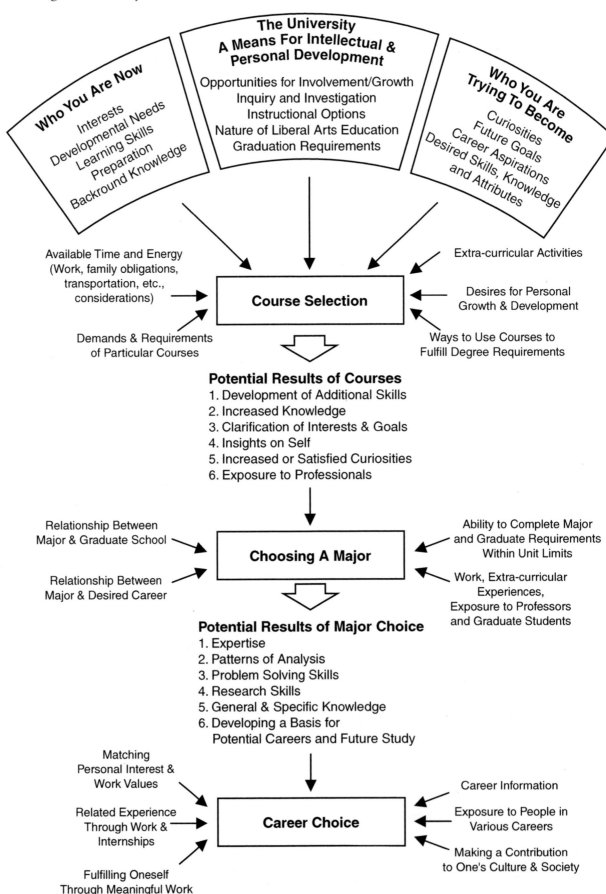

References

Anderson, E. (1988). *Planning for academic success*. Los Angeles: University of California.

Anderson, E. (1997). Advising for excellence. In M. Hovland, E. Anderson, W. McGuire, D. Crockett, J. Kaufman, & D. Woodward (Eds.), *Academic advising for student success and retention* (pp. 161-167). Iowa City, IA: USA Group Noel-Levitz.

Anderson, E. (1995, July). *Strengths-based approaches to promoting student achievement*. Paper presented at the National Conference on Student Retention, New York, NY.

Anderson, E., & McGuire, W. (1996, July). *Spiritual approaches to promoting student persistence*. Paper presented at the National Conference on Student Retention, Orlando, FL.

Astin, A. (1993). *What matters in college? Four critical years revisited*. San Francisco: Jossey-Bass.

Baker, R., McNeil, O., & Siryk, B. (1985). Expectation and reality in freshman adjustment to college. *Journal of Counseling Psychology, 32*(1), 94-103.

Bandura, A. (1982). Self-efficacy mechanism in human agency. *American Psychologist, 37*(2), 122-147.

Cross, P. (1999). What do we know about student learning, and how do we know it? *Innovative Higher Education, 23*(4), 255-70.

Herzberg, F. H. (1987, September/October). One more time: How do you motivate employees? *Harvard Business Review*, 53-60. (Reprinted from *Harvard Business Review*, January/February 1968).

Juillerat, S. (2000, February). *The neglected sophomore*. Paper presented at the 19th Annual Conference on The First-Year Experience, Columbia, SC.

Lawler, E. E., III. (1991). The design of effective reward systems. In R. M. Steers & L. W. Porter (Eds.), *Motivation and work* (pp. 507-530). New York: McGraw-Hill.

Lemons, L., & Richmond, D. (1987). A developmental perspective of sophomore slump. *NASPA Journal, 24*(3), 15-19.

Locke, E. A., & Latham, G. P. (1990). *A theory of goal setting and task performance*. Englewood Cliffs, NJ: Prentice Hall.

Schreiner, L. (1996, July). *Who stays, who leaves, and why*. Paper presented at the National Conference on Student Retention, Orlando, FL.

Schreiner, L. (1999, March). Focus groups conducted with sophomores at Eastern College. Unpublished data.

Steele, C. (1999). Race and the schooling of black Americans. In M. H. Davis (Ed.), *Social psychology annual editions*. Guilford, CT: Dushkin/McGraw-Hill.

Tinto, V. (1987). *Leaving college*. Chicago: The University of Chicago Press.

From Drift To Engagement: Finding Purpose And Making Career Connections In The Sophomore Year

by Philip D. Gardner

Chapter 6

"Her focus was diffuse. Her motivation for why she was there seemed unclear. She felt rudderless."

J. J. Abrams, co-creator of the hit WB series *Felicity*, provided the above rationale for why the number of viewers fell during the show's sophomore season in 1999-2000 ("Viewers Teach Felicity Lessons After Sophomore Slump, Relationship Returns"). But Abrams' description of main character Felicity Porter could easily be applied to many college sophomores—they lack focus, their motivations are not clearly defined, and they are often drifting through their second year without direction.

This chapter opens with a discussion of a study conducted by the author between 1994 and 1997, focusing on how students acquire the non-content competencies needed to survive and thrive in college and in the world of work. While results of the study are being used to develop preliminary models of how students acquire skills and competencies, the discussion in this chapter will focus primarily on a comparison of student engagement across class levels as revealed through the process of conducting this study. The sophomores described here appear to be moving to a different place in regard to engagement from where they started as first-year students or from where they will end as seniors. The key findings suggest that these sophomores, like the character of Felicity Porter, appear to be drifting—not entirely committed to their academic endeavors nor engaged in organizations and activities available to them. The drift can be described as a lack of meaningful relationships with faculty, staff, or mentors, a mismatch in learning strategies, or poorly defined purposes for being in college. Helping students create connections between academic study and future career goals may provide them with the rudder they need to steer themselves through college. The second half of this chapter will propose strategies for creating connections to and between academic and career goals.

Background

Recent research by Ernest Pascarella, Patrick Terenzini, and others has contributed to our understanding of how curricular and co-curricular activities and experiences enhance gains in academic knowledge (Springer, Terenzini, & Pascarella, 1995 and Terenzini, Pascarella, & Blimling, 1996). Similarly, success in the workplace depends on a set of skills that serve as companions to academic competencies. These skills are often referred to as people skills or non-content competencies and include teamwork, interpersonal communication, personal accountability, and applied problem solving (Secretary's Commission on Achieving Necessary Skills, 1991). The Collegiate Employment Research Institute initiated a project, modeling Pascarella and Terenzini's work on learning and cognitive development, to determine how students acquire or develop these non-content competencies. That study is described in greater detail below.

Participants

The initial phase of this study, conducted at a large, public university in the Midwest, focused on juniors and seniors. During the second phase, participants were selected from the first-year and sophomore classes. Students were mailed personalized letters requesting their participation; in addition, faculty were asked to

volunteer their classes (some offered extra credit). Student organizations were invited to participate. Participants were asked to view a video and then complete a survey. A total of 2,825 students viewed the workplace skills video; of these 2,414 completed a college engagement survey that could be used for statistical purposes. Approximately 34% of the respondents who identified their class level were first-year students and sophomores, approximately 18% and 16% respectively. Juniors and seniors equally split the remaining 66% of respondents who provided class-level information. The lower rate of participation by sophomores may be explained by two factors. First, few courses cater exclusively to sophomores, making it difficult to find a large number of these students in one place. Furthermore, sophomores are not likely to have joined student professional organizations in their respective colleges, again adding to the difficulty of attracting them to the study.

Based on selected student characteristics (grade point average, gender, and academic major), the class-level cohorts in this study reflected the characteristics of their class levels in the university at large. The only deviation from the university student profile concerned race. While a comparable percentage of minorities viewed the video, they completed the questionnaire at a lower rate than other students.

Instrument

Two instruments were administered to each student. Students first watched a 60-minute video, containing 35 workplace vignettes, which covered issues new college graduates might encounter in their first job after graduation. Each vignette embedded the non-content competencies identified earlier. At the conclusion of the video, participants were given the 10-page student engagement survey. To obtain their assessment results, interpretation packet, and portfolio, students were required to return the survey within two weeks (85% completed the survey).

The student engagement survey contained a number of items that covered academic course patterns, classroom interactions, learning styles, extracurricular participation, interactions with faculty outside of class, allocation of time to various activities during a given week, and measurements of five major personality factors. Specifically, the survey included:

1. *Workplace competencies*. Developed by Employment Technologies Corporation (2000), a series of workplace vignettes assesses the viewer's use of certain skills in context. These assessments provide normed referenced results as well as feedback on the appropriate use for each competency.
2. *Course-taking patterns*. Self-reported tallies of courses taken and those currently left to take can be used to determine concentration and breadth of study.
3. *Learning styles*. The True Colors (Lowry, n.d.) self-assessment of teaching and learning styles (a word sort exercise) offers a cursory examination of the primary approach a student uses to engage in learning.
4. *Study methods*. The researches adopted Bloom's (1956) taxonomy of learning approaches.
5. *Ambiguity and mastery*. Scales that regarded dealing with ambiguity and level of mastery in academic and non-academic skills were included in the instrument.
6. *Personality measures*. The researchers used the NEO Personality Inventory Revised (Costa & McCrae, 1991) to measure selected dimensions of personality.
7. *Classroom interactions*. A series of questions, asking about classroom participation with faculty and other students, was designed.
8. *Out-of-class interactions*. Participants responded to questions concerning contacts with faculty and peers outside of class on certain topics.
9. *Extracurricular participation*. A check list of types and levels of participation in co-curricular activities was included.
10. *Weekly time allocation*. Participants completed a chart of time usage for a typical week including class, studying, leisure, and sleep.
11. *Personal and academic development*. Self-reported measures of development and the impact of faculty, peers, and extracurricular activities on development were collected.

The Drift

Based on the information drawn from the survey on campus and classroom activities, several aspects of sophomore engagement and learning vary markedly from students at other class levels. These sophomores made behavioral choices, moving away from the learning environment established as first-year students toward more self-indulgent activities. In general, they showed more disengagement from coursework, fewer hours spent in pursuit of academic responsibilities, and more time involved in socializing and peer-related activities. The following sections highlight several key areas of sophomore life.

Learning Styles

Schroeder (1993) highlights the learning style (modalities) differences between faculty and students. Learning style assessments have become widely used in a variety of classroom settings. Indeed, some faculty have adjusted their course deliveries to accommodate multiple learning styles. However, additional insight into what happens to different types of learners as they move from first-year to senior status is minimal. Results of our research highlight the urgency for more in-depth studies on learning styles.

In this study, students were grouped by their dominant learning style preferences. Approximately 15% were identified as abstract/logical learners who dealt well with theory and abstraction, willingly explored new knowledge (often on their own), pursued learning because of intrinsic interests, and involved themselves in critical thinking. Another 15% were sensitive, performing learners who needed highly interactive and creative environments where instructors were likely to have open communication styles. These students tend to congregate in the performing and fine arts, telecommunications, and graphics. From the first to the senior year, these two learning styles were represented by approximately the same percentage in each class, with abstract learning increasing slightly across the four years.

One third of the students starting their first year could be described as practical, passive learners who desired clearly defined goals, detailed course outlines and lessons, emphasis on assigned texts, and focus on specific course content. Learning in this sense can be viewed as cyclical: It is initiated by the instructor, and received and returned (via tests) by the student. This study suggests the number of passive learners increases over time, comprising 40% of the class by the senior year.

The remaining one third can be characterized as hands-on learners who want direct, immediate application of what they have learned. They like to be involved in co-curricular experiences, simulations, and enjoyable activities. The composition of the first-year and sophomore classes is approximately the same regarding hands-on learners. A dramatic change occurs in the junior and senior years, characterized by a 10% drop in the number of hands-on learners in the junior year and an additional 5% drop in the senior year. By the senior year, hands-on learners comprise barely 15% of the class.

What happened to these learners? This study was not designed as a longitudinal exercise; thus no individual changes can be measured. However, two theories seem plausible:

1. *Adoption*. Hands-on learners may use another learning style, most likely the practical-passive style. As the dominant teaching modality used in colleges and universities, the adoption of practical-passive learning may be best viewed as a survival technique. However, by adopting this technique, there is no guarantee that the students are engaged learners.

2. *Leaving*. Unable to find a learning method that works for them, some students may opt to leave the university, usually after the sophomore year. The learning style incompatibility may be masked by bad grades and certainly a lack of connection to academics. A correlation between learning styles and leaving cannot be established with certainty at this point. This is an incentive for additional research in this area.

The revealing fact is that the loss of hands-on learners begins at the end of the sophomore year. These types of learners may attempt to find ways to become engaged; however, they may also spend more time drifting through courses. The challenge is to place them in situations where they can use their dominant learning style to their advantage. With hands-on learners comprising the largest segment of the population, an institution's ability to retain students may rest on their ability to accommodate these types of learners better.

Learning Approaches

How students approach learning may determine whether they actually realize the institution's desired learning outcomes. Baxter-Magolda (1992) presents four stages of learning. Beginning in the "dependent stage" (absolute knowing) where students rely on the instructor for knowledge, students move through "transitional" and "independent" stages before reaching "contextual learning" situations. As a student moves through these phases, knowledge emerges from sources other than the instructor, including peers and one's self. In the contextual phase, knowledge is integrated, compared, applied, and judged depending on the situation. Baxter-Magolda indicates that the slow movement of students through these phases is particularly striking;

by the completion of their senior year, few of the students she studied had passed through Phase 2.

In seeking a formal way to measure Baxter-Magolda's learning transition, Bloom's taxonomy (1956) was adopted. Bloom identified six levels of learning:

1. *Memorizing*: learning specific ideas, words, or methods so that you can remember them the same way
2. *Interpreting*: mentally putting ideas in different terms—to translate, reorganize, and extend one's thinking based on principles
3. *Applying*: drawing upon a variety of concepts and applying them to problems or situations
4. *Analyzing*: breaking material into parts, detecting relationships among the parts, and understanding why they are organized in a particular way
5. *Synthesizing*: organizing ideas into new relationships or structures, integrating information from diverse sources
6. *Evaluating*: making judgments about the value of concepts, theories, evidence, and methods

Sophomores reported that they allocated the largest amount of their time to memorizing material. When asked to rank their preferred strategy for learning academic material, more than 60% listed memorizing as either their first or second choice. All students gave preeminence to memorizing and interpreting strategies, but sophomores were less likely than students in other class levels to employ applying or analyzing strategies in their learning.

Sophomores apparently take on a low-maintenance learning strategy. Memorizing and interpreting have been strongly reinforced during high school. Even though first-year students appeared to be engaged in higher-level learning strategies, sophomores slid back into old habits that often carried through to

the senior year. Their preferred strategies required the least engagement in academic endeavors.

Classroom Interactions

Students were asked a series of questions about the frequency of different interactions—instructor to student, student to instructor, student to student, and individual involvement—taking place in the classroom. While faculty were sometimes reported to praise and encourage students in class or built upon student-generated ideas, sophomores were more likely to view the instructor as seldom or never interacting with students. Furthermore, sophomores were less likely to see other students engaging in class. Not only were students seldom participating in class, sophomores perceived much less student-to-student interaction.

More striking were the responses about their own levels of participation. Nearly 30% said they never or seldom participated in class discussion; 42% said they did sometimes. When they responded to a question from the instructor, their response was usually information they had memorized. Sophomore respondents were significantly less involved in interactions with other students.

The picture that emerges from this series of questions on academic engagement is that this group of sophomores is passively involved in their learning. They are doing little to initiate their own learning, and they do not perceive that their instructors are engaged with them. The drift into a passive learner only begins to turn around during the senior year.

Faculty Contact Outside Class

Looking at reported interactions of at least 10 minutes with faculty outside of class, sophomores reported the fewest number of encounters. More than half of the sophomores never contacted a faculty member about a course concern or intellectual issue, while 48%

of sophomores occasionally sought out a faculty member to discuss an advising issue. When sophomores did visit with a faculty member, career issues were most likely to be the topic. During the second year, students appear to begin searching for direction by soliciting advice from faculty members.

Even though the level of communication between sophomores and faculty is low, the differences among class levels are not dramatic. Only seniors appear to seek out faculty with some regularity. The number of contacts with faculty and staff on campus, except in work situations, is negligible. In several companion studies examining student interactions, students said they seldom communicated with academic, student affairs, or administrative staff. Most of a student's time is spent among peers. By the sophomore year, the drift away from faculty and staff is noticeable; movement back starts in the senior year when students solicit assistance on their job search.

Peer Interactions

The nature of peer interactions takes on added dimensions during the sophomore year. During the first year, 53% of respondents said conversations focused constantly on courses, and 54% of respondents said conversations focused on personal problems constantly. In the sophomore year, courses drop as a point of discussion only to be picked up again once students have been admitted to their majors. Sophomores were reported to spend dramatically less time discussing personal problems and campus issues, focusing instead on career and major concerns. For sophomores, as they testified in comments, confirming their major selection or deciding on an appropriate career was their biggest personal problem. At this point, sophomores were verifying their decisions and making purposeful connections between their academics and life after graduation. They drew assistance in resolving these issues primarily from their peers.

Non-Academic Activities

All of the college students surveyed said they spend the majority of their non-academic time hanging out with friends. Sophomores, however, spent significantly more time at parties and visiting local bars, even though most were under the legal drinking age. Over 60% described their frequency of involvement in the party scene as "fairly often to constantly." This figure was 10% above the same level of involvement for all other classes. Another way to approach the time spent partying was to look at the percentage of time not involved. Only 17% of the sophomores reported not being engaged in partying, compared to approximately 26% for each of the other classes.

In gathering data on students' use of time over a typical week, a weekly log of their time was collected. Sophomores spent considerably less time doing academic activities, including studying, outside of class than first-year students and juniors (approximately 15%, compared to 18% to 20% for the others, respectively). Sophomores exceeded their classmates in time spent pursuing social activities, leisure, and physical fitness. Sophomores seem to carve out a significant portion of their time (25%) for self-gratifying activities. The apparent cause for a 20% decrease in these activities during the junior and senior years is the dramatic increase in the amount of time spent participating in paid employment.

Satisfaction with Institution

A series of questions examined various aspects of personal and intellectual development and personal satisfaction with the university. Sophomores reported that students and student organizations were competitive at a slightly higher level than other class levels. Overall they described their peers as friendly and supportive.

While 53% of the second-year students found

their faculty members approachable and helpful, this represented an 18% decline from what first-year students reported. While juniors and seniors held comparable views on the helpfulness of faculty as sophomores, they were less likely than sophomores to describe faculty as remote and unsympathetic. Juniors, in particular, were more positive about the support received from their faculty. See Juillerat's chapter in this monograph for a more in-depth exploration of satisfaction issues among sophomores.

In terms of intellectual and personal growth, students from all class levels attributed the positive strides they were making to their peers. And while most students (approximately 73% across class levels) noted a positive contribution to their intellectual development by faculty, sophomores took a slightly more neutral view. Faculty influence on personal development and satisfaction with the institution was perceived as minimal.

Faculty were largely absent from students' perceptions of their personal growth. About one third said they felt faculty made a positive contribution, 10% said a negative contribution, and the remainder remained neutral. Again, sophomores held a more neutral (less positive) position than other classes regarding their faculty members' contribution. A similar pattern emerged when the focus shifted to institutional satisfaction.

Re-Directing Drift

Based on the results of this study, sophomores have created their own unique biosphere. A complex mix of individual and group behavioral choices appear to be pushing this sphere along a path running counter to the academic path of the engaged learner. The degree to which the sphere drifts from the institution's preferred path depends on the institution's ability to pull it back into a prescribed orbit. The pull depends on what curricular and institutional structures can be put in place to engage sophomores and to

allow their experiences to give direction to their lives. Some suggestions for correcting this drift in the areas of learning, purpose, linkages, and connections are made below.

Learning

Appreciation for diverse learning styles is growing; however, it may not be possible to accommodate multiple learning styles in every class. What can be incorporated are activities that allow the student to apply learning in context. One proven method is learning through service (Zlotkowski, 1997–1998; Zlotkowski, 1998). When faculty incorporate service in their courses and take time to reflect periodically on the service activity, they increase opportunities for student engagement by illustrating or elaborating on theoretical constructs. Service learning is particularly appropriate for sophomores who may not have enough experience to obtain career-related employment.

Internships, which have been properly structured around learning objectives, could also be used with sophomores. Juniors and seniors usually pursue internships to gain work experience to enhance their job prospects. For sophomores, a reflective internship would involve not only an out-of-class experience, but also a reflective session (through journals and group discussion), emphasizing the connection between theory and application.

A good place to start is right on campus. Many on-campus jobs can serve as vehicles for reflective internships. The connections are obvious in some assignments, such as computer support, laboratory assistants, and information specialists in the library. With some creativity and realignment of expectations, jobs in the cafeteria, maintenance department, and janitorial service can also create unique reflective opportunities. These positions can be used to improve customer service skills, management of logistics, multi-tasking, and other important competencies.

These competencies are frequently discussed in business and planning courses, for example. These more experiential approaches to learning may also help sophomores resolve those questions about career and major highlighted earlier.

Commitment and Connections

Some sophomores will make connections to the campus on their own, with seemingly little effort. Others will struggle; of these, some students will follow their peers while others will falter and give up (Hines, 1999). Schneider and Stevenson (1999) have labeled this generation of American teenagers the "Ambition Generation," qualifying the label by adding "directionless." Confused about where they want to go and unsure how their academic work relates to their future, sophomores become anxious, frustrated and overly cautious in dealing with their academic and post-graduation plans. Many options for assisting sophomores with their particular needs are offered throughout this monograph.

One such approach to mitigate frustration would be to insert a sophomore experience course that bridges the first year and formal entry into a major. A sophomore course would build upon the first-year course where the focus is on adjusting to and succeeding in college. The course would prepare students for the major and the senior capstone course where additional attention may be given to job-search strategies, interviewing skills, and contract negotiations. What better connection for a sophomore who is confused and directionless than interacting with a mentor who can discuss a research topic or special issue, showing how their scholarship links to the real world. In addition, faculty can help their seminar participants shape their own world.

Several institutions, including *West Virginia University, Michigan State University*, and the *University of Guelph* (Ontario, Canada) offer sophomore seminars. While developed independently, these courses all share several critical elements.

1. *Values clarification and purpose*. By the sophomore year, students are beginning to take ownership of their values, which may raise conflict with their reasons for attending the university. By assisting them in their value clarification process, educators can give attention to the students' commitment to learning and to the connection between academic endeavors and career interests. The culminating exercise is the development of a personal mission statement that provides the focus for sustaining their journey through college and into the workplace.
2. *Competency development*. Critical skills and competencies that students will need in their personal and professional lives are identified and discussed. Exercises often provide the students with an understanding of the skills components. Attention is given to how these skills and competencies can be developed through curricular and co-curricular activities.
3. *Occupational interest*. Exploration of career interests allows students to clarify their interests, as well as align their academic and work aspirations. The activities in this section introduce the concept of career and potential career options available in today's economy. For many students this becomes the first time they have been challenged to make a career commitment. Career services staff could provide excellent guidance in leading these exploration exercises.

Hersch (1999), in her study of youth, *A Tribe Apart*, documents the disconnect between adults and American teenagers. Upon entering college, first-year students encounter a number of "adults" in various capacities. These encounters are brief and seldom repeated unless the student seeks them out. The only constant adult interaction these newly emerging adults experience is with faculty. Students matriculate believing that faculty will be an integral part of their lives. In reality, few students actually connect with a faculty member, especially on large campuses.

For the sophomore, faculty relationships are even more tenuous. On many campuses, no faculty are designated specifically to interact with sophomores. Sophomores, even though they may have already declared a major, are in a no-man's land: caught between first-year faculty and major faculty who may only recognize their existence when they officially enter a major as a junior.

Creating Linkages to Career

Many avenues exist for students to become involved in campus life. From service to professional organizations, the numbers can be staggering. The number only increases when personal interest groups are included. In the study reported earlier, respondents showed little inclination to join or participate in these groups. Juniors and seniors were more likely to attend professional organizations associated with their majors, yet it is important to draw younger students into these organizations.

Two groups on campus may be important in helping sophomores make connections to career goals. The tendency of sophomores in this study to seek out faculty regarding career issues may suggest the importance of involving faculty in career services designed with sophomores in mind. In this study, sophomores said they also spent time discussing career and major concerns with their peers, suggesting a potentially untapped resource for many campuses. Where possible, colleges and universities should formalize these contacts with faculty and peers to enhance the delivery of career services for sophomores.

Career services can assist students with connecting to opportunities related to the students' interests. The rapid change in the structure of the workplace, in methods for job posting, and in campus recruitment is reshaping program delivery in career services. Schools, like the University of Northern Iowa, are shifting their focus away from job placement to career development. This shift is warranted on two levels:

1. Students need to be prepared earlier for the realities of the workplace. As career services staff lose control of job placement to online options, their efforts are being redirected toward helping students prepare for job entry by focusing on skills, competencies, and practical experiences (i.e., internships and co-op assignments).
2. Career services can assist in the seamless advising initiatives being implemented on campuses, by helping advisors and students, particularly sophomores, align academic study with potential careers.

Of course, career specialists are only able to help those sophomores who avail themselves of the services provided in career centers. A five-pronged strategy for connecting these students to career centers is offered by the University of Cincinnati's Linda Bates Parker (2000), who suggests the following:

1. Conduct sophomore focus groups either online or in person at the career center to determine what these students need. This process can help identify what career service, program, or support would be most valuable to students. A survey may also be conducted to determine the concerns and special needs of these students.
2. Develop a plan for addressing sophomores' specific career planning needs. In a time of limited resources, it is important to identify potential sources of revenue and opportunities for collaboration with other student affairs staff, college advisors, or faculty members.
3. In developing a sophomore-focused plan, the career services specialist should consider activities that compete for these students' time and interest. As noted above, these activities, including socializing, work, family, church, and studying, are plentiful. A successful career services strategy acknowledges that other activities are an important part of the sophomore life and works with, not against, those activities.

4. As noted earlier, infiltrate the sophomore's peer group by collaborating with students in organizations, in classes, and by attending other campus events. Any model for working with sophomores can be pre-tested in these forums.
5. Saturate the marketplace using every creative means possible to attract the targeted audience.

Career development is critical to sophomores as they attempt to decide upon or reaffirm an academic major. What is called for is a multifaceted program that permits (a) exploration of career options, (b) development of a career decision plan, (c) an understanding of the realities of the workplace, and (d) the awareness of co-curricular experiences that enhance the students' career choices. Career centers provide resources that can be integrated into several of the options previously discussed. The key in all venues is to provide a platform where sophomores can develop connections between their academic endeavors and life-long aspirations.

Conclusion

Whether due to a failure to connect with faculty, an inadequate linkage between academic study and career, or a poorly defined purpose, drift appears to cause sophomores to disengage from the institution. Some will drop out; others will persist passively. Efforts to retain first-year students may prove futile if not sustained during the sophomore year. To form a solid foundation for engaged learning, faculty and administrators should visualize a first- and second-year experience. Appreciating differences in learning styles, forging career connections, and defining academic purpose comprise the central focus of this experience. Stopping drift and improving engagement will take a concerted, collective effort by faculty, students, and staff.

References

Baxter-Magolda, M. B. (1992). *Knowing and reasoning in college: Gender related patterns in students' intellectual development*. San Francisco: Jossey-Bass.

Bloom, B. S. (1956). *The taxonomy of educational objectives*. New York: Longmans, Green.

Costa, P. T., Jr., & McCrae, R. R. (1991). *NEO Personality Inventory Revised*. [Survey instrument]. Odessa, FL: Psychological Assessment Resources.

Employment Technologies Corporation. (2000). *Workskills 2000*. [Survey instrument] Altamonte Springs, FL: Author.

Hersch, P. (1999). *A tribe apart: A journey into the heart of American adolescence*. New York: Ballantine Books.

Hines, T. (1999). *Rise and fall of the American teenager*. New York: Baros Books.

Lowry, D. (n.d.). *True colors*. [Survey Instrument]. Corona, CA: Center for Educational Development for True Colors.

Parker, L. B. (2000). *The sophomore year and career issues*. University of Cincinnati (OH).

Schneider, B. L., & Stevenson, D. (1999). *The ambitious generation: America's teenagers motivated but directionless*. New Haven, CT: Yale University Press.

Schroeder, C. C. (1993). New students – new learning styles. *Change, 25*, 21-26.

Secretary's Commission on Achieving Necessary Skills. (1991). *What work requires of* schools. *Executive summary*. Washington, DC: U.S. Department of Labor.

Springer, L., Terenzini, P. L., & Pascarella, E. T. (1995). Influence on college students' orientations toward learning for self-understanding. *Journal of College Student Development, 36*, 5-18.

Terenzini, P. L., Pascarella, E. T., & Blimling, G. S. (1996, March/April). Students' out-of-class experiences and their influence on learning and cognitive development. *Journal of College Student Development*, 49-62.

Viewers teach Felicity lessons after sophomore slump, relationship returns. (2000, June 20). *USA Today*, Life Section, p 1.

Zlotkowski, E. (Ed.). (1997–1998). *AAHE series on service-learning in the disciplines*. Washington, DC: American Association for Higher Education.

Zlotkowski, E. (1998). *Successful service-learning programs: New models of excellence in higher education*. Boston, MA: Anker.

Institutional Approaches to Helping Sophomores

by Scott E. Evenbeck, Michael Boston, Roxanne S. DuVivier, and Kaylene Hallberg

Chapter 7

Academic achievement and persistence to graduation are central issues for institutions of higher education, with retention and graduation rates generally used as benchmarks by which campuses determine whether there is cause for concern. Our experience of high attrition rates at one large urban university led to a heightened concern for the sophomore student. Attrition data for this institution (Office of Information Management and Institutional Research, 1999) are listed in Table 1 on the following page.

While one-year retention rates for sophomores are about 15% higher than for first-year students, the rate for these students continuing another year is still only two of every three students. The National Center for Educational Statistics (Horn, 1998) reports that nearly 30% of beginning students in 1989-1990 left post-secondary education before their second year. Sixteen percent of the students enrolled in the four-year sector left while 42% of those enrolled in the two-year sector left. While some educators may argue that these departures are a short-term problem (i.e., these students have merely stopped out), longitudinal studies conducted five years out show that 35% of the four-year departers stayed out. Moreover, 50% of the two-year departers stayed out. While many students elected for varying reasons to suspend their education, departure for others results in permanent termination of their higher education.

Shifting Institutional Focus to the Sophomore Student

Faculty, staff, and student leadership have traditionally focused on first-year students and seniors—on welcoming students to the academy

Table 1

Attrition Data

	First-Year Students				Sophomores		
Year	Number	No. Retained	Percentage	Number	No. Retained	Percentage
1994	5536	2831	51.14%	4951	3277	66.19%
1995	6062	3215	53.04%	4891	3320	67.88%
1996	6582	3358	51.02%	4899	3301	67.38%
1997	6581	3361	51.07%	5073	3434	67.69%
1998	7045	3530	50.11%	5198	3450	66.37%

and helping them make the transition to college study and later to graduate or professional school or to a career. In our experience, campuses generally allow sophomores to be served by "normal" processes, not by any special efforts to continue their engagement in learning.

Our conceptions of students are the following:

First-Year Students

These students, often called freshmen but now more often inclusively referred to as entering students or as first-year students, have received much attention. The majority of college students are not the full-time, traditional-aged students who fit our traditional characterizations of "students." Demographic trends, especially in population-growth areas, show huge increases in the numbers of nontraditional students. Campuses are seeking creative and effective ways to deal with the diversity of these students. Models developed for 18-year-old white male students often are not effective with the diverse students who now come to our campuses, particularly when delivered by non-diverse faculty and staff. National leadership continues to provide resources for serving these students. Models for first-year

seminars, learning communities, and so on—and the contexts for articulating the principles which are important and for assessing their effectiveness—are critical for our continuing to improve work with these students.

The high attrition rates among first-year students, particularly among minority students, demand our continuing, and increased, attention. Campuses are responding to calls to "front-load" services, to develop resources and strategies for orienting and serving these entering students.

Sophomores

Sophomore students, like first-year students, are also students in transition. These are students who are beyond their first year of study but not yet solidly in their majors on the "graduation track." Students in the first year know that they are new. The institutions know they are new. And, institutions have responded with a variety of strategies to connect students with the campus and to put them "on track" for graduation.

We may even characterize the first-year experience for some students as an introductory "honeymoon" phase where the freshness of the experience is associated with a certain euphoria. As students settle into the daily demands of college life, that euphoric feeling dissipates as what was novel becomes routine. Questions begin to emerge relative to personal satisfaction with the academic experiences and comfort within the college environment. Students who report experiencing a sophomore "let-down" describe a discrepancy between their expectations of college life and the realities of college experience (See Juillerat's chapter in this monograph.).

Students reporting general feelings of malaise approaching their sophomore years have not fully integrated themselves into the fabric of campus life. Unlike their persisting classmates, they have not arrived at a sense of self that allows them to conclude with certainty that higher education is where they want to be. According to Candace Vancko (DuVivier, 1999a), President of SUNY Delhi, a two-year institution in the state of New York, "Students leave for a variety of reasons, but almost all are predicated on their belief that it is more valuable to do something else with their time and money than to return to school. They do not see the second year as having significant value for them." These issues of related value apply to both two-year and four-year students whose lives are affected by financial constraints.

Even the word we use for second-year students has a negative connotation. Sophomoric is defined as "of, befitting, or characteristic of a sophomore; pretentious; immature, juvenile; crude, superficial" (Simpson & Weiner, 1989). Higher education, through first-year programming, has institutionalized support for students, recognizing that student outcomes are a function of the student and of the institution. Yet, with sophomores and students in the transition into the major, there is an implied judgment that the students themselves are primarily responsible for their success or lack thereof.

Juniors and Seniors

There are clearly many first-year and second-year students who are on track to graduate. In highly selective institutions, the overwhelming majority of all students do graduate, often in four years. In many other institutions where Astin (1999) calls on American higher education to take on the development of students' talent and the challenge of serving under-prepared students, the attrition rates in the first year and in the second year are, as noted earlier, in need of improvement. Data reflect, however, that a point exists where students are on track to graduate: where the commitments they have made and the work they have completed, along with the consequences they anticipate associated with graduation; the family, peer, and other support for graduation; and their commitment to see it through, make it likely that a very high proportion of students will graduate.

The work of the institution for these students is supporting them as they make the transition to their next step, be it employment or further study. Colleges and universities have developed senior seminars and other means of supporting students for leaving the institution. Franklin College in Indiana, for example, has a senior residence hall where students are "polished" for graduation, where academic and support services help them complete their academic careers and focus on their next steps.

Evaluating the Sophomore Experience

Our first recommendation would be systematic and sustained evaluation of the sophomore experience. For example, Boston and DuVivier (1999) conducted focus groups on the campus of a major land grant university to gather anecdotal examples of how this institution handled the concerns of sophomores. They summarized the student experience as follows:

At Purdue University, sophomores in residence describe the importance of the transition from the freshman to the sophomore year. They highlight a process by which students move from being defined in the eyes of their parents to deciding what is best for themselves. They indicate that the freshman year provides opportunity for self-analysis and that from this analysis comes a new commitment to self-determination. As students seek to define themselves they begin to make choices affecting their future.

As part of the goal clarification process, parental role shifts from being primary in the decision-making process to that of valued coach. A new set of mentors is acquired who hold positions of influence and professional prominence. The outcome of this developmental process, often emerging during the sophomore year, may result in a change of major, a change of institution, departure from college, or a renewed commitment to the original enrollment goal.

The focus group was conducted with students from various academic, geographic, and socio-economic backgrounds. Their only two commonalties were that they lived in University Residences and the fact that they were upperclass students (sophomore or higher). Other than these factors, the participants were quite varied in their profiles. Focus group data suggest four factors important in dealing with sophomores:

Self-Analysis

These sophomores can be said to have been in a period of self-analysis. They used the resources such as career interest inventories and personality inventories. Their behavior might be called developing a mental map for the future. The students were developing ownership for their academic and vocational decisions. As described earlier in this monograph, Baxter Magolda's (1992) analyses suggest that successful university students do move through such reflection as they mature as students.

Self-Determination

The focus group results further suggest that students move from self-analysis to self-determination. The successful students then move to an articulation of commitment to their course of study. Students on this residential campus did not want to return home and be considered "academic failures." Interestingly, all of the focus group participants said that they influenced their own decisions more than anybody else did; they did not believe themselves to be overly influenced by peers and/or parents.

Clarification of Goals

Students who are successful move from self-analysis and self-determination to clarification of goals in terms of higher education and define their expectations for the future. According to this research they go through a sometimes arduous task of goal setting.

Confirmation from Peers and/or Parents:

Finally, the focus group participants sought confirmation from parents and/or peers.

There is need for additional qualitative and quantitative analysis at the campus level. For example, on a large urban university campus, data for continuing students revealed differences in the pattern of responses for sophomores as compared with first-year students and with the undergraduate population in general (IMIR 1998, 1999). Sophomores rated both the overall quality of instruction and courses in their major areas as significantly more important than did the first-year students. As students are successful in selecting majors and moving into their curricula, it is heartening to find such confirmation of purpose. On the other hand, first-year students and sophomores did not differ in their reported satisfaction with their academic and social experiences, or with their satisfaction with the quality or the faculty or the quality of academic programs.

Sophomores did not differ from the overall undergraduate population on these measures. They did rate the quality of teaching by faculty in their areas as significantly less important than did undergraduates overall. Perhaps access to the major is still more important than the standard of instruction to sophomores.

Issues Impacting the Sophomore Experience

Clearly, coming to college and preparing to leave are important transitions. Yet another transition is maturing from the initial excitement about being in college to being "solidly" in one's major and on track for graduation. In her thoughtful analysis of knowing and reasoning in college, Baxter Magolda (1992) characterizes knowing in the sophomore year as "transitional knowing," consistent with our suggestion that mid-year students are in transition. With transitional knowing, students are moving from absolute knowledge in their first years through transitional knowing to independent knowing and contextual knowing during their last two years. Baxter Magolda bases her analysis on her interviews with 101 students at Miami University over five years. She argues that "incorporating the relational component is the key to transforming education. Acknowledging that knowing is relational and acting on that assumption entail uniting experience and knowing, teaching and learning, students and their peers, and curricular and cocurricular education" (Baxter Magolda, p. 392). The mid-year students are moving toward more independence in their ways of knowing. Their reliance on authority, on absolute knowledge, is giving way to their increased involvement in their own learning. This is all the more reason to find and implement specific programs for supporting these sophomore students.

In addition, as programs are built and policies are implemented specifically targeting the needs of sophomores, a number of student sub-populations deserve focused attention. The general characteristics of these populations do, of course, cut across all class levels, but we contend their intersection with the sophomore year is a particularly tenuous moment in the undergraduate career. For example:

Transfer students. Adelman's (1999) recent research confirms the very high and increasing multiple affiliations of American students. No longer do students go to one institution and graduate from that institution. Students are increasingly consumers of higher education, seeking the contexts and institutions that are most appropriate for their educational needs. Incoming transfers, whether from community colleges or other institutions, are an important component in thinking about sophomores. Issues of course and program articulation are beyond the scope of this chapter; however, important general questions include: How does an institution celebrate its general education program for beginning students, and how is this translated to transfer students? Does orientation exist for new and transfer students? Are there special efforts to connect new and transfer students with the campus and its student services?

Minority students. Blake, Saufley, and Cowan (1973) talk of the "ultimate doom" syndrome. For many minority and first-generation students, there are subtle and sometimes overt messages that some students are not expected to succeed: It is just a matter of time, according to this concept, before these students figure out they do not belong, buy into that fallacy, and leave. Blake, Saufley, and Cowan argue that this syndrome becomes stronger for students as they approach graduation. Attrition rates for all minority students exceed those of "majority" students and suggest the need for continuing attention. Adelman suggests that continual enrollment of minority students is disproportionately important for minority students. Minority students who leave are less likely to return than majority students are

(Adelman, 1999). There must be intentional programming to support continual enrollment and connection with the campus for minority students. These efforts, which may begin in the first year, should be continued into the second year and beyond.

Commuter students. Astin (1993) states that it is often disruptive for a residential student to leave campus. New friendships and expectations and self-concepts reinforce the student as a student on a particular campus. He says, on the other hand, that it is often disruptive for a commuting student to come to campus. Such students have homes, jobs, volunteer commitments, friendships, and other obligations already in place. Coming to school, particularly with all the demands not supported by the ongoing contexts of students' lives, is disruptive to these students. The most straightforward way to restore their lives to "normal" can be for these students to leave campus. The sophomore experience for commuter students becomes more, not less, complicated than the first-year experience. Successful institutional interventions will recognize this.

Impacted majors. The University College Deans and Directors group (Strommer, 1993) has called attention to the importance of supporting students who are seeking impacted majors, those with capped enrollments or high standards for entry into programs. Sophomores are the most likely to face this issue. Admission to college often does not guarantee admission to a particular degree program, whether or not structural arrangements (e.g., separate academics unit for entering students) reinforce that step-wise movement into a major and toward graduation. The advising chapter in this volume calls attention to the importance of advising for sophomores. Institutional attention is also required in defining pathways to graduation for students who are admitted to the institution but who may not qualify for admission into their desired degree program. If the student's first-choice major is not

feasible, then the institution has an obligation to help define and support alternate pathways to graduation.

Community membership. According to Tinto (1993), "the social and intellectual life of most institutions has a center and a periphery" (p. 60). Students who make a successful sophomore adjustment find themselves compatible with the dominant culture or subculture of the campus. Those who describe themselves as marginally involved in the campus culture are more likely to experience a loss of motivation, resulting in poor performance or departure.

For example, *Hocking College*, a two-year technical institution in the foothills of southern Ohio, has found that students are more likely to stay in school if the courses they are taking are challenging and relevant to what they believe to be their ultimate goals. Students at Hocking College (Outreach and Connections Staff, 1999) report experiencing the sophomore slump when requirements feel burdensome or when students feel disconnected from their areas of greatest interest. John Light (DuVivier, 1999b), president of Hocking College, believes "we can eliminate or greatly reduce the sophomore slump by building inclusive campuses with revisioned curriculum tying core requirements closely with majors and by providing opportunity for action-oriented direct experience as a continual part of the educational process."

Best practices. It is imperative that institutions be intentional in implementing best practices for sophomores. Attention to first-year students and seniors with seminars (often in the form of University 101 courses for first-year students and capstones for seniors) should be complemented with curricular innovations designed for sophomores, especially those which emphasize active learning. *Portland State University*, for example, in its innovative curriculum continues the work of the first year with interdisciplinary courses in the sophomore year. Other practices (e.g., service learning in the first-year seminar) should be programmed for sophomores as well. Involvement in undergraduate research should not wait for upper division students fully engaged in their majors but rather should be extended to sophomores. The systematic assessment of attitudes should include not merely first-year and senior year students in the national comparisons; rather, they should include systematic assessments of students in each year of study.

Attention to the curriculum, to career planning, to student life, and to all facets of the college experience are as critical for sophomores as they are for first-year students and for seniors. The institution's response should be grounded in the experience of the students served by that institution. The development of programs or services not based in a firm understanding of the context and of the students themselves will not likely succeed.

Conclusions and Recommendations

In summary, the institutional response to sophomores should be as carefully constructed, intentionally executed, and thoroughly evaluated as the response to the first-year experience has been. Facets of this response should include those described above, and the design of interventions should be informed by the following observations of Boston and DuVivier (1999):

- Students are much less likely to slump if their expectations of college are consistent with college realities.

- Students are less likely to experience a sophomore slump if they feel connected to the dominant campus culture or a specific subculture and are invested in its functions.

- Family support for continuing in college minimizes the likelihood that a slump will result in departure.

- Slumps caused by diminished motivation can be reduced through curricular and co-curricular approaches that actively engage students and maintain interest.

- Residence halls offer a unique opportunity to connect students to the dominant culture and to provide support for intellectual and psychosocial development.

- Sophomores may be particularly primed to begin focused career and life-planning activity.

The following are specific strategies for beginning the process of building an institutional response to sophomores:

- *Focus Sessions.* Conversations with students, convened early, give them a voice. Students themselves are able to challenge assumptions, their own and those of the campus leadership, as they develop programs to serve them. Students may pose questions and receive answers on topics of importance to them. This process sets the stage for active participation in the college experience and fosters a habit of personal involvement. Sophomores engaged in such a process can provide insights into the first-year experience as well as help craft a meaningful and effective second-year experience.

- *Academic Choice.* Students should get good information about career choices, with the ability to see how curricular choices do or do not provide flexibility in moving toward a degree. As noted earlier, when majors or courses are not available to all students, institutions are obliged to help students select or design other options for their degrees that are consistent with personal interests and scholastic aptitudes.

- *Exploration of Self.* Campuses need to encourage and formalize the process of self-analysis as a necessary introductory step in the process of personal and academic growth. According to Lisa Tetzloff (Boston & DuVivier, 1999), Director of Residence Life at Purdue University, "sophomores are almost an invisible group ... neither new enough nor experienced enough to draw our attention." Paying particular attention to the developmental needs of this overlooked student population will yield significant benefits in our pursuit of fostering student success.

To paraphrase the Greek philosopher Epictetus (1996), "we are not at fault if we are uninformed... but once we know of a problem and have considered it ... we are at fault if we do nothing."

Attending to the learning of all our students, including sophomores, and developing programs, in context, to serve them, should result in improved academic achievement and increased persistence levels of among these important students.

References

Adelman, C. (1999). *Answers in the toolbox: Academic intensity, attendance patterns, and bachelors degree attainment*. Washington, DC: National Institution on Postsecondary Education, Libraries, and Lifelong Learning. (ERIC Document Reproduction Service No. ED 431 363)

Astin, A. (1999). Rethinking academic "excellence." *Liberal Education, 85* (2), 8-18.

Astin, A. (1993). *What matters in college*. San Francisco: Jossey-Bass.

Baxter Magolda, M. B. (1992). *Knowing and reasoning in college: gender-related patterns in students' intellectual development*. San Francisco: Jossey-Bass.

Blake, H. J., Saufley, R. W., & Cowan K. (1973). The struggles of minority students at predominately white institutions. In J. F. Noonan, J. Cones, & D. Jahna (Eds.) *Teaching minority students*. San Francisco: Jossey-Bass.

Boston, M., & DuVivier, R. S. (1999). *The sophomore slump: Institutional issues*. [Internal Report]. West Lafayette: Purdue University.

DuVivier, R. S. (1999a, November 5). Telephone interview with Candace Vancko.

DuVivier, R. S. (1999b, November 9). Telephone Interview with John Light.

Epictetus. (1996). *Epictetus*. Cambridge, MA: Harvard University Press.

Horn, L. (1998). *Stopouts or stayouts? Undergraduates who leave college in their first year*. Washington, DC: National Center for Education Statistics. (ERIC Document Reproduction Service No. ED 425 683)

Office of Information Management and Institutional Research (IMIR) Indiana University Purdue University Indianapolis. (1998). *IUPUI entering student Survey, fall 1998 administration*. Retrieved from the World Wide Web: http://www.imir.iupui.edu.

Office of Information Management and Institutional Research (IMIR) Indiana University Purdue University Indianapolis. (1999). *1999 continuing student satisfaction and priorities survey*. Retrieved from the World Wide Web: http://www.imir.iupui.edu.

Outreach and Connections Staff. (1999). *Attrition timeline study*. [Internal report]. Nelsonville, OH: Hocking College.

Simpson, J. A. & Weiner, E. S. C. (1989). *Oxford English Dictionary* (2nd ed.) (Vols. 1-20). New York: Oxford University Press.

Strommer, D. (1993). Not quite good enough: Drifting about in higher education. *AAHE Bulletin, 45* (10).

Tinto, V. (1993). *Leaving college: Rethinking the causes and cures of student attrition* (2nd ed.). Chicago: The University of Chicago Press.

Summary and Recommendations

by John N. Gardner, Jerry Pattengale and Laurie A. Schreiner

Chapter 8

The purpose of this chapter is to provide a summary of the monograph and to present the recommendations of those who provided the impetus for this monograph. Because of his continued focus on improving the first college year, one of the authors, John Gardner, was frequently asked when he planned to invest his time and energy in addressing the sophomore year. In fact, Gardner had long been looking for a way to address the question of whether the sophomore slump existed, when in 1998, he discovered two scholars researching attrition in the small, Christian, liberal arts college sector.

Jerry Pattengale and Laurie Schreiner, of Indiana Wesleyan University and Eastern College respectively, were trying to address what they regarded as a real and troubling phenomenon concerning sophomores. Their work led to a partnership to produce this monograph and to a commitment by Gardner and The National Resource Center for The First-Year Experience and Students in Transition at the University of South Carolina to publish their findings and recommendations.

The main purpose of this chapter is to summarize their conclusions and to suggest ways to address the issues and concerns surrounding the sophomore experience.

Findings

1. We find that there are some unique issues for sophomores and that these issues demand further exploration.

2. Further, and perhaps more importantly, we find that the sophomore slump should be a compelling academic and programmatic issue for all institutions, especially those that manifest unacceptably high levels of attrition among second-year students.

3. The most acute manifestation of the sophomore slump is

premature dropping out of college on the part of students who have not been able either to develop or attain satisfactory progress toward educational goals.

4. Other symptoms of the sophomore slump may include, but are not limited to: prolonged indecisiveness about selecting a major, inappropriate decision making about academic course selection and major and minor fields of study, low levels of academic engagement, low levels of commitment, dysfunctional behavior which interferes with academic success (such as excessive drinking), disappointment and frustration with the academic experience, increased time-to-degree completion rates, absenteeism, lack of co-curricular involvement, and lack of social and academic integration.

5. In our work on the sophomore slump, we have uncovered several important myths regarding this phenomenon, which may actually serve to prevent its being adequately recognized and/or addressed. The first myth is that "the retention problem" is primarily a problem of the first year; and the second is that if we concentrate retention programming on the first year, we will have adequately addressed the problem, to the extent that it can be addressed at all. The third myth is that once a student gets through the first year, he or she is "over the hump," that the toughest part is over. Our findings imply, to the contrary, that significant attrition continues through and at the conclusion of the sophomore year. Thus, a campus that "front loads" all retention programming and resources in the first year will not have adequately addressed the problem. Because sophomore attrition is a concern, we are quite clearly not yet "over the hump" at the end of the first year.

6. We find that sophomores experience a unique transition with some similarities to the first-year transition, but there are also some marked differences. As Boivin, Fountain, and Baylis point out in their chapter, sophomores are "between" in every respect. They are no

longer naïve about the college experience; yet they may not be fully engaged in it, so cynicism and disillusionment may result. They often have not committed to a specific major, yet they may be painfully aware of what they are not interested in or good at doing. They have "survived" the first year, yet they may not be given leadership opportunities or ways of becoming more involved with faculty similar to those offered upper-level students. Having weathered the storms of personal transition issues in the first year, many sophomores are now keenly aware of what higher education "ought" to be doing for them. As a result, they may judge the adequacy of an institution and find that it does not meet their needs.

Juillerat's chapter in this monograph highlights the increased expectations which sophomores have for service excellence, high-quality advising and teaching, having a voice on campus, and a campus climate of care and concern for them. The increased expectations in these areas seem to parallel the personal developmental needs of sophomores: the need for achieving competence, developing autonomy, establishing identity, and developing purpose. The critical issue in the sophomore year appears to be that of developing a sense of meaning and purpose—about one's education, one's career, and one's life goals.

7. We find consensus among the chapter authors, other researchers, and higher education practitioners with whom the authors have conducted focus groups that the issues and variables in students' lives that correlate positively with the sophomore slump are more of a personal developmental than an academic nature.

8. Research on factors influencing the sophomore slump suggests a consensus on the most likely culprits. These factors center around inadequate academic advising; lack of integration between academic advising and career planning; low levels of academic and

social integration; insufficient levels of interaction between faculty and students outside the classroom; disillusionment with the large general education classes of the first year; lack of a sufficient number of classes in the major in the first and second year and thus the failure to begin a process of intellectual engagement in the major; and the withdrawal of classic first-year experience support initiatives prematurely, i.e., at the end of the first year, before students have become appropriately committed and intellectually engaged to ensure successful degree completion and goal attainment.

9. We find that a sizable number and variety of programs already in place, especially in baccalaureate-level institutions, both public and private, attempting to address the phenomena of the sophomore slump. We find these initiatives are relatively recent and largely lacking in sufficient assessment evidence to make any kind of claim of effectiveness in terms of utility and impact.

Recommendations

1. While the sophomore slump has been satisfactorily identified, there are insufficient data and research describing the phenomenon. Therefore, we would challenge educational researchers to pay more attention to this critical transition during the undergraduate experience when students are making extremely important decisions: What are they going to study; where are they going to study and with whom; and will they remain in college at all?

2. We recommend that not only institutions but also professional associations interested in improving undergraduate education pay more attention to the sophomore year—groups such as the American Association for Higher Education, the Association of American Colleges and Universities, the National Academic Advising Association, National Association for Developmental Education, Association for Institutional Research, etc.

3. Regardless of what may be going on at the national level, the most important task for educators is to collect data from sophomores regarding their experiences on the local campus level. Institutions should use this data to answer a set of key questions:

a. What are the differences between first- and second-year dropouts?

b. What are the challenges facing second-year students on your campus?

c. What are you doing to address these problems now?

d. How do you either continue or withdraw certain types of first-year experience support initiatives after the first year?

e. Who is responsible for the academic advising of second-year students on your campus? What are the advising systems, structures, and practices for sophomores? How well is this system working?

f. What kind of connections do sophomores have to faculty on an out-of-class basis, given that out-of-class student-faculty interaction has proven to be essential for increasing intellectual engagement and student persistence?

g. What is the linkage of your sophomore-year advising approach to an intentional career planning process?

h. Is there a connection between your campus's sophomore slump phenomenon and your own general education curriculum? Are students primarily or exclusively "getting general education courses out of the way?" To what extent are your students able to begin significant intellectual experiences in their major by the sophomore year?

4. The consensus of scholars in this monograph is that the variables related to the sophomore slump are multiple and complex. Therefore, we believe that in order to assist students in dealing with these issues, a holistic approach is essential. A complex interplay exists between both academic and personal developmental variables that must be addressed simultaneously. Such complexity requires a deliberate academic and student affairs partnership to address the sophomore slump.

5. We believe that the key personal developmental issue on the part of sophomore students is the fundamental question of the development of purpose. In order to achieve this, students must have positive, successful, and intellectually engaging academic experiences. Further, they need access to well-integrated advising and career planning services, which can help them connect coursework to major, career, and life goals.

6. This leads us to argue that perhaps the most important recommendation we can offer is the need for intentionality. Once you recognize the legitimacy of concerns regarding sophomores, it is important that you not leave key sophomore year developmental and academic outcomes to chance. Instead, you must address them deliberately and intentionally.

7. We believe that increasing opportunities for faculty-student mentoring relationships outside of the classroom will help ease the sophomore slump.

8. We also believe that a key issue for sophomores is increasing their level of intellectual engagement in order to sustain the high expectations of the first year. The focus on intellectual engagement has to be coupled with the development of a true general education model that spans all four years, instead of the classic distribution model which encourages students to think of getting "those large, dull classes that are not really related to what I wanted to learn" out of the way. A coherent, sequenced core curriculum containing common courses designed specifically for the sophomore year is a goal worthy of consideration.

9. Given that four out of five American college and university students are in the public sector, we believe that the phenomenon of the sophomore slump deserves even more attention, especially in light of findings (see Juillerat's chapter in this monograph) suggesting lower levels of satisfaction and higher student expectations for service excellence, faculty availability, and advising in the public sector. Of particular concern to us within the public sector is inattention to the sophomore slump phenomenon in the American community college. Further, because the majority of students who enter college in the United States begin in the two-year sector and because attrition is highest in the two-year sector, more attention to the sophomore slump in the community college context is long overdue.

10. To the extent that college students have a successful first-year experience that includes effective academic advising, intentional linkage with career planning, development of positive relationships with faculty, academic and social integration with peers, and good progress toward the development of purpose, students will be more likely to experience success in the sophomore year and remain enrolled in college. Thus, the first-year remains the most vital period of the overall undergraduate experience for increasing retention and graduation rates. The first-year experience is the most important foundation for ameliorating the effects of the sophomore slump. This is not to say that this kind of emphasis in and of itself will alleviate or prevent the sophomore slump. What we are arguing for in this monograph is a complementary relationship with an empowering first-year experience providing the basis for the sophomore year and a continuation and expansion of the number of

initiatives beyond the first year. We reiterate that educational programmers focusing on the sophomore year should give priority to academic advising, career planning, out-of-class faculty-student interactions, and academic and social integration with one's peers. Toward those ends, we recommend especially the continuation beyond the first year of the very promising learning community concept which has been successful in increasing intellectual engagement, faculty-student contact, peer-to-peer interaction, and academic and social integration. We also recommend the incorporation of advising and career planning into expanded learning community programs. Further, we recommend the inclusion of more intentional practice of the classic American "support group" intervention. We have developed all kinds of successful "support groups" for first-year students, and we believe that this certainly can and must be done for second-year students.

Conclusion

In conclusion, we wish to underscore the wisdom of fellow chapter author Jerry Gaff, who contends that whenever "scholars focus on a particular kind of student, such as college sophomores, and seek ways to assure that those individuals receive an effective college education, the remedies recommended turn out to be good education—not just for the particular group identified, but for all students" (p. 47). Thus, the kind of intensified focus we have argued for in this monograph on such strategies as improved academic advising and career planning, more faculty-student contact outside of class, more academic and social integration for peers, must not be addressed entirely in isolation by focusing exclusively on this cohort of sophomores. These practices are valuable, and we believe must be provided for all undergraduate students. They must precede and continue through the sophomore year and beyond.

We note some parallels here with the beginning of the national dialogue on the topic of "the freshman year experience" in the early 1980's. The first step toward increasing the focus of educators on this important educational transition and challenge was to provide a language both to describe the phenomenon and an intellectual rationale for taking it seriously. At the very least, we are hopeful that by devoting this monograph to the topic of sophomores, we will have encouraged the academic worthiness of an intensified campus-based examination of the existence of the sophomore slump phenomenon and possible programmatic interventions to ameliorate its negative consequences. We wish our readers all the best on this important new effort to improve the educational experience of American college and university undergraduates.

Assessing The Expectations And Satisfactions of Sophomores: The Data

by Stephanie Juillerat

A
Appendix

The Student Satisfaction Inventory (SSI), a 73-item instrument that assesses a large number of areas related to the college experience, was administered to 118,706 traditional undergraduate students (72,245 from private colleges and 44,461 from public colleges) in the 1998–1999 academic year. In order to answer the question "what makes sophomores unique?", a number of analyses were conducted to compare public and private college sophomores to members of other class levels or groups. In all of these comparisons, one of two basic statistical techniques was used: a comparison of score rankings or a test of statistical differences in score values. The second analysis, the test of statistical difference, utilizes either a t-test or analysis of variance (ANOVA) to determine if one group's (usually sophomores) score on an item is significantly higher or lower than another group's score on the same item ($p < .05$). See Chapter 2 for an in-depth discussion of the methods and results of this study.

to tables

Table 1

A Comparison of Private and Public College Sophomores on Issues of Importance (N=23,848)

		Private (*n*=16,059)		Public (*n*=7,789)	
	Item	Score	Rank	Score	Rank
8.	The content of courses within my major is valuable.	6.65*	1	6.56	1
16.	The instruction in my major field is excellent.	6.63*	2	6.52	3
68.	Nearly all of the faculty are knowledgeable in their field.	6.58*	3	6.50	4
58.	The quality of instruction I receive in most of my classes is excellent.	6.55*	4	6.48	6
66.	Tuition paid is a worthwhile investment.	6.52*	5	6.40	10
34.	I am able to register for classes I need with few conflicts.	6.51*	6	6.55	2
17.	Adequate financial aid is available for most students.	6.47*	7	6.28	17
39.	I am able to experience intellectual growth here.	6.47*	7	6.33	14
33.	My academic advisor is knowledgeable about requirements in my major.	6.46*	9	6.50	4
7.	The campus is safe and secure for all students.	6.45	10	6.45	8
69.	There is a good variety of courses provided on this campus.	6.42*	11	6.46	7
25.	Faculty are fair and unbiased in their treatment of individual students.	6.42*	11	6.36	12
55.	Major requirements are clear and reasonable.	6.41*	13	6.38	11
29.	It is an enjoyable experience to be a student on this campus.	6.39*	14	6.27	18
41.	There is a commitment to academic excellence on this campus.	6.39*	14	6.22	22

table continues

	Item	Private (n=16,059)		Public (n=7,789)	
		Score	Rank	Score	Rank
6.	My academic advisor is approachable.	6.39*	14	6.42	9
65.	Faculty are usually available after class and during office hours.	6.38*	17	6.35	13
26.	Computer labs are adequate and accessible.	6.37*	18	6.30	15
2.	The campus staff are caring and helpful.	6.36*	19	6.25	19
59.	The institution shows concern for students as individuals.	6.36*	19	6.19	26
12.	Financial aid awards are announced to students in time to be helpful in college planning.	6.31*	21	6.14	32
45.	Students are made to feel welcome on this campus.	6.29*	22	6.13	33
5.	Financial aid counselors are helpful.	6.27*	23	6.02	42
14.	My academic advisor is concerned about my success as an individual.	6.26	24	6.24	20
51.	This institution has a good reputation within the community.	6.26*	24	6.06	38
47.	Faculty provide timely feedback about student progress in a course.	6.25*	26	6.21	23
72.	On the whole, the campus is well-maintained.	6.24*	27	6.19	26
3.	Faculty care about me as an individual.	6.24*	27	6.05	41
36.	Security staff respond quickly in emergencies.	6.24	27	6.23	21
57.	I seldom get the "run-around" when seeking information on this campus.	6.22*	30	6.17	30
18.	Library resources and services are adequate.	6.21	31	6.20	25

table continues

	Item	Private (n=16,059)		Public (n=7,789)	
		Score	Rank	Score	Rank
49.	There are adequate services to help me decide upon a career.	6.21	31	6.18	28
11.	Billing policies are reasonable.	6.18*	33	6.10	35
23.	Living conditions in the residence halls are comfortable (adequate space, lighting, heat, air conditioning, telephones, etc.)	6.17*	34	5.87	54
4.	Admissions staff are knowledgeable.	6.17	34	6.18	28
27.	The personnel involved in registration are helpful.	6.17	34	6.15	31
53.	Faculty take into consideration student differences as they teach a course.	6.16*	37	6.07	36
28.	Parking lots are well-lighted and secure.	6.13*	38	6.21	23
61.	Adjunct faculty are competent as classroom instructors.	6.12*	39	6.01	43
35.	The assessment and course placement procedures are reasonable.	6.10*	40	6.06	38
67.	Freedom of expression is protected on campus.	6.09*	41	6.00	45
50.	Class change (drop/add) policies are reasonable.	6.07*	42	6.13	33
71.	Channels for expressing student complaints are readily available.	6.06*	43	5.94	48
63.	Student disciplinary procedures are fair.	6.06*	43	5.88	52
73.	Student activities fees are put to good use.	6.05	45	6.07	36
48.	Admissions counselors accurately portray the campus in their recruiting practices.	6.05*	45	5.77	60

table continues

	Item	Private (*n*=16,059)		Public (*n*=7,789)	
		Score	Rank	Score	Rank
44.	Academic support services adequately meet the needs of students.	6.02*	47	5.95	47
62.	There is a strong commitment to racial harmony on this campus.	6.02*	47	5.88	52
21.	The amount of student parking space on campus is adequate.	6.01*	49	6.30	15
22.	Counseling staff care about students as individuals.	6.00*	50	5.92	50
38.	There is an adequate selection of food available in the cafeteria.	5.98*	51	5.71	64
32.	Tutoring services are readily available.	5.97	52	5.99	46
19.	My academic advisor helps me set goals to work toward.	5.96*	53	6.01	43
64.	New student orientation services help students adjust to college.	5.95*	54	5.81	57
20.	The business office is open during hours which are convenient for most students.	5.95	54	5.92	50
10.	Administrators are approachable to students.	5.94*	56	5.81	57
43.	Admissions counselors respond to prospective students' unique needs and requests.	5.93*	57	5.85	55
1.	Most students feel a sense of belonging here.	5.92*	58	5.62	65
37.	I feel a sense of pride about my campus.	5.92*	58	5.72	62
40.	Residence hall regulations are reasonable.	5.91*	60	5.54	68
60.	I generally know what's happening on campus.	5.88*	61	5.72	62

table continues

	Item	Private (n=16,059)		Public (n=7,789)	
		Score	Rank	Score	Rank
70.	Graduate teaching assistants are competent as classroom instructors.	5.88*	61	6.06	38
15.	The staff in the health services area are competent.	5.86*	63	5.94	48
46.	I can get easily involved in campus organizations.	5.81*	64	5.75	61
13.	Library staff are helpful and approachable.	5.80*	65	5.85	55
54.	Bookstore staff are helpful.	5.80	65	5.78	59
30.	Residence hall staff are concerned about me as an individual.	5.76*	67	5.35	71
52.	The student center is a comfortable place for students to spend their leisure time.	5.75*	68	5.60	66
56.	The student handbook provides helpful information about campus life.	5.70*	69	5.60	66
42.	There are a sufficient number of weekend activities for students.	5.45*	70	5.36	70
31.	Males and females have equal opportunities to participate in intercollegiate athletics.	5.43	71	5.44	69
24.	The intercollegiate athletic programs contribute to a strong sense of school spirit.	5.26	72	5.26	72
9.	A variety of intramural activities are offered.	4.88*	73	4.96	73

Note: * indicates a statistically significant difference between the two groups ($p < .05$).

Table 2

A Comparison of Private and Public College Sophomores on Issues of Satisfaction (N=23,848)

	Item	Private (*n*=16,059)		Public (*n*=7,789)	
		Score	Rank	Score	Rank
68.	Nearly all of the faculty are knowledgeable in their field.	5.73*	1	5.49	1
51.	This institution has a good reputation within the community.	5.72*	2	5.33	4
39.	I am able to experience intellectual growth here.	5.55*	3	5.31	5
8.	The content of courses within my major is valuable.	5.53*	4	5.27	7
65.	Faculty are usually available after class and during office hours.	5.53*	4	5.34	3
72.	On the whole, the campus is well-maintained.	5.51*	6	5.40	2
7.	The campus is safe and secure for all students.	5.50*	7	5.21	9
16.	The instruction in my major field is excellent.	5.46*	8	5.17	12
41.	There is a commitment to academic excellence on this campus.	5.45*	9	5.03	21
33.	My academic advisor is knowledgeable about requirements in my major.	5.45*	9	5.27	7
6.	My academic advisor is approachable.	5.43*	11	5.13	15
45.	Students are made to feel welcome on this campus.	5.42*	12	5.08	16
55.	Major requirements are clear and reasonable.	5.41*	13	5.08	16
2.	The campus staff are caring and helpful.	5.41*	13	4.91	32
58.	The quality of instruction I receive in most of my classes is excellent.	5.38*	15	5.06	19

table continues

	Item	Private (n=16,059)		Public (n=7,789)	
		Score	Rank	Score	Rank
13.	Library staff are helpful and approachable.	5.33*	16	5.18	11
29.	It is an enjoyable experience to be a student on this campus.	5.32*	17	5.16	13
3.	Faculty care about me as an individual.	5.30*	18	4.64	50
32.	Tutoring services are readily available.	5.26*	19	5.04	20
46.	I can get easily involved in campus organizations.	5.24*	20	4.96	26
59.	The institution shows concern for students as individuals.	5.20*	21	4.63	53
14.	My academic advisor is concerned about my success as an individual.	5.20*	21	4.83	35
50.	Class change (drop/add) policies are reasonable.	5.19*	23	5.01	23
56.	The student handbook provides helpful information about campus life.	5.18*	24	4.94	27
27.	The personnel involved in registration are helpful.	5.17*	25	4.81	38
54.	Bookstore staff are helpful.	5.17	25	5.14	14
1.	Most students feel a sense of belonging here.	5.16*	27	4.94	27
31.	Males and females have equal opportunities to participate in intercollegiate athletics.	5.16*	27	5.03	21
4.	Admissions staff are knowledgeable.	5.16*	27	4.79	39
62.	There is a strong commitment to racial harmony on this campus.	5.13*	30	4.87	33
37.	I feel a sense of pride about my campus.	5.12*	31	4.94	27
25.	Faculty are fair and unbiased in their treatment of individual students.	5.11*	32	4.86	34

table continues

| Item | Private (n=16,059) | | Public (n=7,789) | |
	Score	Rank	Score	Rank
64. New student orientation services help students adjust to college.	5.11*	32	4.79	39
35. The assessment and course placement procedures are reasonable.	5.08*	34	4.78	41
60. I generally know what's happening on campus.	5.06*	35	4.64	50
69. There is a good variety of courses provided on this campus.	5.05*	36	5.30	6
61. Adjunct faculty are competent as classroom instructors.	5.05*	36	4.83	35
10. Administrators are approachable to students.	5.03*	38	4.68	48
20. The business office is open during hours which are convenient for most students.	5.02*	39	4.78	41
49. There are adequate services to help me decide upon a career.	5.01*	40	4.77	43
44. Academic support services adequately meet the needs of students.	5.01*	40	4.75	44
43. Admissions counselors respond to prospective students' unique needs and requests.	5.00*	42	4.60	54
30. Residence hall staff are concerned about me as an individual.	4.99*	43	4.44	63
47. Faculty provide timely feedback about student progress in a course.	4.96*	44	4.67	49
63. Student disciplinary procedures are fair.	4.92*	45	4.82	37
53. Faculty take into consideration student differences as they teach a course.	4.89*	46	4.52	58
67. Freedom of expression is protected on campus.	4.89*	46	5.08	17

table continues

	Item	Private (n=16,059)		Public (n=7,789)	
		Score	Rank	Score	Rank
22.	Counseling staff care about students as individuals.	4.88*	48	4.55	55
70.	Graduate teaching assistants are competent as classroom instructors.	4.85*	49	4.74	45
48.	Admissions counselors accurately portray the campus in their recruiting practices.	4.84*	50	4.69	46
5.	Financial aid counselors are helpful.	4.84*	50	4.47	62
26.	Computer labs are adequate and accessible.	4.83*	52	4.99	25
34.	I am able to register for classes I need with few conflicts.	4.81*	53	4.40	64
52.	The student center is a comfortable place for students to spend their leisure time.	4.81*	53	4.93	31
9.	A variety of intramural activities are offered.	4.81*	53	5.00	24
18.	Library resources and services are adequate.	4.77*	56	5.19	10
28.	Parking lots are well-lighted and secure.	4.76*	57	4.55	55
19.	My academic advisor helps me set goals to work toward.	4.73*	58	4.50	59
15.	The staff in the health services area are competent.	4.70	59	4.69	46
66.	Tuition paid is a worthwhile investment.	4.70*	59	4.94	27
17.	Adequate financial aid is available for most students.	4.66*	61	4.33	67
12.	Financial aid awards are announced to students in time to be helpful in college planning.	4.66*	61	4.34	66

table continues

	Item	Private (*n*=16,059)		Public (*n*=7,789)	
		Score	Rank	Score	Rank
36.	Security staff respond quickly in emergencies.	4.63	63	4.63	52
40.	Residence hall regulations are reasonable.	4.56*	64	4.49	60
71.	Channels for expressing student complaints are readily available.	4.56*	64	4.35	65
57.	I seldom get the "run-around" when seeking information on this campus.	4.52*	66	4.09	70
73.	Student activities fees are put to good use.	4.48*	67	4.23	68
11.	Billing policies are reasonable.	4.46	68	4.49	60
23.	Living conditions in the residence halls are comfortable (adequate space, lighting, heat, air conditioning, telephones, etc.)	4.46*	68	4.08	72
24.	The intercollegiate athletic programs contribute to a strong sense of school spirit.	4.44*	70	4.54	57
42.	There are a sufficient number of weekend activities for students.	4.29*	71	4.13	69
38.	There is an adequate selection of food available in the cafeteria.	3.92*	72	4.09	70
21.	The amount of student parking space on campus is adequate.	3.71*	73	2.68	73

Note: * indicates a statistically significant difference between the two groups ($p <.05$).

Table 3

A Comparison of Private College Students across Class Level on Issues of Importance (N=74,248)

	Item	First-Year (n=29,398)		Sophomore (n=16,059)		Junior (n=15,391)		Senior (n=13,397)	
		Score	Rank	Score	Rank	Score	Rank	Score	Rank
8.	The content of courses within my major is valuable.	6.58	1	6.65*	1	6.68	1	6.68	1
16.	The instruction in my major field is excellent.	6.52	2	6.63*	2	6.66	2	6.67	2
68.	Nearly all of the faculty are knowledgeable in their field.	6.50	3	6.58*	3	6.58	3	6.60	3
58.	The quality of instruction I receive in most of my classes is excellent.	6.47	4	6.55*	4	6.57	4	6.58	4
66.	Tuition paid is a worthwhile investment.	6.42	6	6.52*	5	6.52	6	6.51	5
34.	I am able to register for classes I need with few conflicts.	6.40	7	6.51*	6	6.54	5	6.51	5
17.	Adequate financial aid is available for most students.	6.43	5	6.47*	7	6.46	8	6.39	15
39.	I am able to experience intellectual growth here.	6.40	7	6.47*	7	6.44	9	6.45	8
33.	My academic advisor is knowledgeable about requirements in my major.	6.38	10	6.46*	9	6.52	6	6.49	7
7.	The campus is safe and secure for all students.	6.40	7	6.45*	10	6.44	9	6.42	11
69.	There is a good variety of courses provided on this campus.	6.36	12	6.42*	11	6.42	13	6.40	14
25.	Faculty are fair and unbiased in their treatment of individual students.	6.36	12	6.42*	11	6.43	11	6.44	9

table continues

		First-Year (n=29,398)		Sophomore (n=16,059)		Junior (n=15,391)		Senior (n=13,397)	
	Item	Score	Rank	Score	Rank	Score	Rank	Score	Rank
55.	Major requirements are clear and reasonable.	6.34	15	6.41*	13	6.41	14	6.41	12
29.	It is an enjoyable experience to be a student on this campus.	6.37	11	6.39*	14	6.35	20	6.30	20
41.	There is a commitment to academic excellence on this campus.	6.34	15	6.39*	14	6.40	15	6.41	12
6.	My academic advisor is approachable.	6.30	19	6.39*	14	6.43	11	6.42	10
65.	Faculty are usually available after class and during office hours.	6.29	21	6.38*	17	6.38	16	6.36	17
26.	Computer labs are adequate and accessible.	6.36	12	6.37	18	6.36	19	6.38	16
2.	The campus staff are caring and helpful.	6.32	17	6.36*	19	6.37	17	6.33	19
59.	The institution shows concern for students as individuals.	6.30	19	6.36*	19	6.37	17	6.36	17
12.	Financial aid awards are announced to students in time to be helpful in college planning.	6.27	22	6.31*	21	6.30	21	6.22	28
45.	Students are made to feel welcome on this campus.	6.31	18	6.29*	22	6.25	26	6.21	29
5.	Financial aid counselors are helpful.	6.19	29	6.27*	23	6.26	25	2.26	24
14.	My academic advisor is concerned about my success as an individual.	6.20	27	6.26*	24	6.30	21	6.29	21

table continues

	Item	First-Year (n=29,398)		Sophomore (n=16,059)		Junior (n=15,391)		Senior (n=13,397)	
		Score	Rank	Score	Rank	Score	Rank	Score	Rank
51.	This institution has a good reputation within the community.	6.21	25	6.26*	24	6.24	27	6.26	24
47.	Faculty provide timely feedback about student progress in a course.	6.18	30	6.25*	26	6.27	24	6.27	23
72.	On the whole, the campus is well-maintained.	6.23	23	6.24*	27	6.19	31	6.17	30
3.	Faculty care about me as an individual.	6.15	34	6.24*	27	6.28	23	6.28	22
36.	Security staff respond quickly in emergencies.	6.20	27	6.24*	27	6.22	30	6.17	30
57.	I seldom get the "run-around" when seeking information on this campus.	6.12	35	6.22*	30	6.23	28	6.23	27
18.	Library resources and services are adequate.	6.16	33	6.21*	31	6.23	28	6.24	26
49.	There are adequate services to help me decide upon a career.	6.22	24	6.21*	31	6.17	33	6.17	30
11.	Billing policies are reasonable.	6.07	39	6.18*	33	6.19	31	6.15	34
23.	Living conditions in the residence halls are comfortable (adequate space, lighting, heat, air conditioning, telephones, etc.)	6.21	25	6.17*	34	6.00	46	5.88	51
4.	Admissions staff are knowledgeable.	6.17	31	6.17*	34	6.15	35	6.10	38
27.	The personnel involved in registration are helpful.	6.17	31	6.17	34	6.16	34	6.14	35

table continues

	Item	First-Year (n=29,398)		Sophomore (n=16,059)		Junior (n=15,391)		Senior (n=13,397)	
		Score	Rank	Score	Rank	Score	Rank	Score	Rank
53.	Faculty take into consideration student differences as they teach a course.	6.12	35	6.16*	37	6.15	35	6.11	37
28.	Parking lots are well-lighted and secure.	6.03	43	6.13*	38	6.15	35	6.13	36
61.	Adjunct faculty are competent as classroom instructors.	6.02	44	6.12*	39	6.13	38	6.17	30
35.	The assessment and course placement procedures are reasonable.	6.10	37	6.10*	40	6.09	39	6.05	39
67.	Freedom of expression is protected on campus.	6.07	39	6.09*	41	6.07	40	6.04	42
50.	Class change (drop/add) policies are reasonable.	6.01	48	6.07*	42	6.03	43	6.00	43
71.	Channels for expressing student complaints are readily available.	5.98	52	6.06*	43	6.06	41	6.05	39
63.	Student disciplinary procedures are fair.	6.02	44	6.06*	43	6.01	45	5.97	45
73.	Student activities fees are put to good use.	6.02	44	6.05*	45	6.02	44	5.97	45
48.	Admissions counselors accurately portray the campus in their recruiting practices.	6.05	42	6.05*	45	6.00	46	5.97	45
44.	Academic support services adequately meet the needs of students.	6.06	41	6.02*	47	5.97	50	5.92	49
62.	There is a strong commitment to racial harmony on this campus.	6.01	48	6.02*	47	6.00	46	5.98	44

table continues

	Item	First-Year (n=29,398)		Sophomore (n=16,059)		Junior (n=15,391)		Senior (n=13,397)	
		Score	Rank	Score	Rank	Score	Rank	Score	Rank
21.	The amount of student parking space on campus is adequate.	5.87	60	6.01*	49	6.06	41	6.05	39
22.	Counseling staff care about students as individuals.	6.02	44	6.00*	50	5.95	51	5.88	51
38.	There is an adequate selection of food available in the cafeteria.	5.97	53	5.98*	51	5.88	54	5.74	59
32.	Tutoring services are readily available.	6.08	32	5.97*	52	5.85	59	5.70	64
19.	My academic advisor helps me set goals to work toward.	5.91	56	5.96*	53	5.99	49	5.93	48
64.	New student orientation services help students adjust to college.	6.00	50	5.95*	54	5.86	58	5.81	55
20.	The business office is open during hours which are convenient for most students.	5.93	54	5.95	54	5.95	51	5.92	49
10.	Administrators are approachable to students.	5.89	58	5.94*	56	5.91	53	5.87	53
43.	Admissions counselors respond to prospective students' unique needs and requests.	6.00	50	5.93*	57	5.88	54	5.79	57
1.	Most students feel a sense of belonging here.	5.86	62	5.92*	58	5.87	57	5.78	58
37.	I feel a sense of pride about my campus.	5.87	60	5.92*	58	5.88	54	5.84	54
40.	Residence hall regulations are reasonable.	5.92	55	5.91*	60	5.73	65	5.62	66

table continues

	Item	First-Year (*n*=29,398)		Sophomore (*n*=16,059)		Junior (*n*=15,391)		Senior (*n*=13,397)	
		Score	Rank	Score	Rank	Score	Rank	Score	Rank
60.	I generally know what's happening on campus.	5.88	59	5.88*	61	5.80	61	5.74	59
70.	Graduate teaching assistants are competent as classroom instructors.	5.91	56	5.88*	61	5.80	61	5.73	61
15.	The staff in the health services area are competent.	5.84	63	5.86*	63	5.80	61	5.71	63
46.	I can get easily involved in campus organizations.	5.83	64	5.81*	64	5.73	65	5.64	65
13.	Library staff are helpful and approachable.	5.75	69	5.80*	65	5.81	60	5.81	55
54.	Bookstore staff are helpful.	5.80	65	5.80*	65	5.75	64	5.73	61
30.	Residence hall staff are concerned about me as an individual.	5.78	67	5.76*	67	5.58	69	5.49	69
52.	The student center is a comfortable place for students to spend their leisure time.	5.80	65	5.75*	68	5.67	67	5.60	67
56.	The student handbook provides helpful information about campus life.	5.76	68	5.70*	69	5.62	68	5.54	68
42.	There are a sufficient number of weekend activities for students.	5.50	71	5.45*	70	5.29	71	5.16	71
31.	Males and females have equal opportunities to participate in intercollegiate athletics.	5.51	71	5.43*	71	5.36	70	5.27	70
24.	The intercollegiate athletic programs contribute to a strong sense of school spirit.	5.30	72	5.26*	72	5.15	72	5.03	72

table continues

Item	First-Year (*n*=29,398)		Sophomore (*n*=16,059)		Junior (*n*=15,391)		Senior (*n*=13,397)	
	Score	Rank	Score	Rank	Score	Rank	Score	Rank
9. A variety of intramural activities is offered.	4.97	73	4.88*	73	4.75	73	4.53	73

Note: * indicates that sophomores differ significantly from at least one other class level ($p < .05$).

Table 4

A Comparison of Private College Students across Class Level on Issues of Satisfaction (N=74,248)

		First-Year (n=29,398)		Sophomore (n=16,059)		Junior (n=15,391)		Senior (n=13,397)	
	Item	Score	Rank	Score	Rank	Score	Rank	Score	Rank
68.	Nearly all of the faculty are knowledgeable in their field.	5.79	2	5.73*	1	5.69	1	5.60	1
51.	This institution has a good reputation within the community.	5.80	1	5.72*	2	5.65	2	5.53	2
39.	I am able to experience intellectual growth here.	5.58	7	5.55*	3	5.53	4	5.48	6
8.	The content of courses within my major is valuable.	5.58	7	5.53*	4	5.52	5	5.43	7
65.	Faculty are usually available after class and during office hours.	5.56	10	5.53*	4	5.52	5	5.50	3
72.	On the whole, the campus is well-maintained.	5.70	3	5.51*	6	5.48	8	5.40	9
7.	The campus is safe and secure for all students.	5.68	4	5.50*	7	5.43	10	5.37	10
16.	The instruction in my major field is excellent.	5.44	16	5.46*	8	5.48	8	5.41	8
41.	There is a commitment to academic excellence on this campus.	5.61	6	5.45*	9	5.39	11	5.27	16
33.	My academic advisor is knowledgeable about requirements in my major.	5.42	17	5.45*	9	5.56	3	5.49	4
6.	My academic advisor is approachable.	5.53	11	5.43*	11	5.51	7	5.49	4
45.	Students are made to feel welcome on this campus.	5.62	5	5.42*	12	5.31	16	5.22	18

table continues

	Item	First-Year (n=29,398)		Sophomore (n=16,059)		Junior (n=15,391)		Senior (n=13,397)	
		Score	Rank	Score	Rank	Score	Rank	Score	Rank
55.	Major requirements are clear and reasonable.	5.48	12	5.41*	13	5.37	13	5.37	10
2.	The campus staff are caring and helpful.	5.58	7	5.41*	13	5.35	14	5.23	17
58.	The quality of instruction I receive in most of my classes is excellent.	5.45	13	5.38*	15	5.39	11	5.32	12
13.	Library staff are helpful and approachable.	5.31	25	5.33	16	5.31	16	5.32	12
29.	It is an enjoyable experience to be a student on this campus.	5.45	13	5.32*	17	5.22	19	5.13	20
3.	Faculty care about me as an individual.	5.36	23	5.30*	18	5.33	15	5.32	12
32.	Tutoring services are readily available.	5.45	13	5.26*	19	5.14	22	5.03	23
46.	I can get easily involved in campus organizations.	5.31	25	5.24*	20	5.18	20	5.14	19
59.	The institution shows concern for students as individuals.	5.42	17	5.20*	21	5.12	23	5.00	27
14.	My academic advisor is concerned about my success as an individual.	5.30	28	5.20*	21	5.28	18	5.29	14
50.	Class change (drop/add) policies are reasonable.	5.27	30	5.19*	23	5.15	21	5.13	20
56.	The student handbook provides helpful information about campus life.	5.31	25	5.18*	24	5.09	26	4.98	30
27.	The personnel involved in registration are helpful.	5.39	20	5.17*	25	5.10	25	5.04	22

table continues

	Item	First-Year (n=29,398)		Sophomore (n=16,059)		Junior (n=15,391)		Senior (n=13,397)	
		Score	Rank	Score	Rank	Score	Rank	Score	Rank
54.	Bookstore staff are helpful.	5.28	29	5.17*	25	5.11	24	5.01	25
1.	Most students feel a sense of belonging here.	5.27	30	5.16*	27	5.09	26	4.99	28
31.	Males and females have equal opportunities to participate in intercollegiate athletics.	5.24	34	5.16*	27	5.08	28	4.99	28
4.	Admissions staff are knowledgeable.	5.40	19	5.16*	27	5.08	28	4.91	34
62.	There is a strong commitment to racial harmony on this campus.	5.38	21	5.13*	30	5.02	34	4.93	31
37.	I feel a sense of pride about my campus.	5.25	32	5.12*	31	5.03	32	4.93	31
25.	Faculty are fair and unbiased in their treatment of individual students.	5.37	22	5.11*	32	5.04	30	4.90	36
64.	New student orientation services help students adjust to college.	5.22	36	5.11*	32	5.03	32	4.91	34
35.	The assessment and course placement procedures are reasonable.	5.22	36	5.08*	34	5.04	30	5.03	23
60.	I generally know what's happening on campus.	5.14	44	5.06*	35	4.93	42	4.79	42
69.	There is a good variety of courses provided on this campus.	5.36	23	5.05*	36	4.94	40	4.88	38
61.	Adjunct faculty are competent as classroom instructors.	5.21	38	5.05*	36	4.98	36	4.90	36

table continues

		First-Year (n=29,398)		Sophomore (n=16,059)		Junior (n=15,391)		Senior (n=13,397)	
	Item	Score	Rank	Score	Rank	Score	Rank	Score	Rank
10.	Administrators are approachable to students.	5.24	34	5.03*	38	4.93	41	4.78	43
20.	The business office is open during hours which are convenient for most students.	5.14	44	5.02*	39	4.96	37	4.86	39
49.	There are adequate services to help me decide upon a career.	5.25	32	5.01*	40	4.95	38	4.80	41
44.	Academic support services adequately meet the needs of students.	5.21	38	5.01*	40	4.95	38	4.86	39
43.	Admissions counselors respond to prospective students' unique needs and requests.	5.20	40	5.00*	42	4.91	43	4.78	43
30.	Residence hall staff are concerned about me as an individual.	5.09	51	4.99*	43	4.81	47	4.69	49
47.	Faculty provide timely feedback about student progress in a course.	5.03	55	4.96*	44	5.02	34	5.01	25
63.	Student disciplinary procedures are fair.	5.13	48	4.92*	45	4.84	46	4.71	48
53.	Faculty take into consideration student differences as they teach a course.	5.06	54	4.89*	46	4.81	47	4.78	43
67.	Freedom of expression is protected on campus.	5.18	41	4.89*	46	4.78	50	4.69	49
22.	Counseling staff care about students as individuals.	5.08	52	4.88*	48	4.85	45	4.75	46

table continues

	Item	First-Year (n=29,398)		Sophomore (n=16,059)		Junior (n=15,391)		Senior (n=13,397)	
		Score	Rank	Score	Rank	Score	Rank	Score	Rank
70.	Graduate teaching assistants are competent as classroom instructors.	5.08	52	4.85*	49	4.73	53	4.61	55
48.	Admissions counselors accurately portray the campus in their recruiting practices.	5.15	42	4.84*	50	4.68	55	4.48	62
5.	Financial aid counselors are helpful.	5.12	49	4.84*	50	4.80	49	4.73	47
26.	Computer labs are adequate and accessible.	5.15	42	4.83*	52	4.66	57	4.55	58
34.	I am able to register for classes I need with few conflicts.	5.14	44	4.81*	53	4.86	44	4.92	33
52.	The student center is a comfortable place for students to spend their leisure time.	5.14	44	4.81*	53	4.69	54	4.53	59
9.	A variety of intramural activities are offered.	4.85	64	5.81*	53	4.76	52	4.68	52
18.	Library resources and services are adequate.	5.12	49	4.77*	56	4.61	61	4.43	64
28.	Parking lots are well-lighted and secure.	4.95	59	4.76*	57	4.68	55	4.62	54
19.	My academic advisor helps me set goals to work toward.	4.85	64	4.73*	58	4.78	50	4.69	49
15.	The staff in the health services area are competent.	4.91	61	4.70*	59	4.65	59	4.60	56
66.	Tuition paid is a worthwhile investment.	5.01	56	4.70*	59	4.65	58	4.60	56

table continues

	Item	First-Year (n=29,398)		Sophomore (n=16,059)		Junior (n=15,391)		Senior (n=13,397)	
		Score	Rank	Score	Rank	Score	Rank	Score	Rank
17.	Adequate financial aid is available for most students.	4.99	57	4.66*	61	4.62	60	4.63	53
12.	Financial aid awards are announced to students in time to be helpful in college planning.	4.99	57	4.66*	61	4.61	61	4.53	59
36.	Security staff respond quickly in emergencies.	4.87	63	4.63*	63	4.53	63	4.46	63
40.	Residence hall regulations are reasonable.	4.69	68	4.56*	64	4.51	64	4.49	61
71.	Channels for expressing student complaints are readily available.	4.90	62	4.56*	64	4.43	65	4.29	67
57.	I seldom get the "run-around" when seeking information on this campus.	4.93	60	4.52*	66	4.38	69	4.21	70
73.	Student activities fees are put to good use.	4.80	66	4.48*	67	4.32	70	4.18	71
11.	Billing policies are reasonable.	4.73	67	4.46*	68	4.42	66	4.33	66
23.	Living conditions in the residence halls are comfortable (adequate space, lighting, heat, air conditioning, telephones, etc.)	4.56	70	4.46*	68	4.42	66	4.43	64
24.	The intercollegiate athletic programs contribute to a strong sense of school spirit.	4.59	69	4.44*	70	4.39	68	4.28	68
42.	There are a sufficient number of weekend activities for students.	4.43	71	4.29*	71	4.28	71	4.27	69

table continues

	Item	First-Year (n=29,398)		Sophomore (n=16,059)		Junior (n=15,391)		Senior (n=13,397)	
		Score	Rank	Score	Rank	Score	Rank	Score	Rank
38.	There is an adequate selection of food available in the cafeteria.	4.15	72	3.92*	72	3.90	72	4.00	72
21.	The amount of student parking space on campus is adequate.	4.06	73	3.71*	73	3.60	73	3.53	73

Note: * indicates that sophomores differ significantly from at least one other class level ($p < .05$).

Table 5

A Comparison of Public College Students across Class Level on Issues of Importance (N=44,461)

	Item	First-Year (*n*=16,165)		Sophomore (*n*=7,789)		Junior (*n*=9,868)		Senior (*n*=10,639)	
		Score	Rank	Score	Rank	Score	Rank	Score	Rank
8.	The content of courses within my major is valuable.	6.46	2	6.56*	1	6.60	1	6.62	1
34.	I am able to register for classes I need with few conflicts.	6.48	1	6.55*	2	6.59	3	6.58	3
16.	The instruction in my major field is excellent.	6.40	8	6.52*	3	6.60	1	6.62	1
33.	My academic advisor is knowledgeable about requirements in my major.	6.46	2	6.50*	4	6.55	4	6.57	4
68.	Nearly all of the faculty are knowledgeable in their field.	6.45	4	6.50*	4	6.53	5	6.54	5
58.	The quality of instruction I receive in most of my classes is excellent.	6.41	7	6.48*	6	6.53	5	6.53	6
69.	There is a good variety of courses provided on this campus.	6.44	5	6.46	7	6.46	8	6.43	10
7.	The campus is safe and secure for all students.	6.43	6	6.45	8	6.47	7	6.44	8
6.	My academic advisor is approachable.	6.39	9	6.42	9	6.45	9	6.45	7
66.	Tuition paid is a worthwhile investment.	6.35	11	6.40*	10	6.45	9	6.44	8
55.	Major requirements are clear and reasonable.	6.34	12	6.38*	11	6.43	11	6.41	11
25.	Faculty are fair and unbiased in their treatment of individual students.	6.34	12	6.36*	12	6.40	12	6.41	11

table continues

	Item	First-Year (n=16,165)		Sophomore (n=7,789)		Junior (n=9,868)		Senior (n=10,639)	
		Score	Rank	Score	Rank	Score	Rank	Score	Rank
65.	Faculty are usually available after class and during office hours.	6.31	14	6.35*	13	6.38	14	6.38	13
39.	I am able to experience intellectual growth here.	6.31	14	6.33	14	6.35	15	6.34	16
21.	The amount of student parking space on campus is adequate.	6.08	37	6.30*	15	6.39	13	6.38	13
26.	Computer labs are adequate and accessible.	6.24	18	6.30*	15	6.32	16	6.37	15
17.	Adequate financial aid is available for most students.	6.26	17	6.28*	17	6.25	19	6.18	25
29.	It is an enjoyable experience to be a student on this campus.	6.36	10	6.27*	18	6.22	25	6.15	26
2.	The campus staff are caring and helpful.	6.21	23	6.25	19	6.25	19	6.23	23
14.	My academic advisor is concerned about my success as an individual.	6.23	19	6.24	20	6.25	19	6.24	22
36.	Security staff respond quickly in emergencies.	6.28	16	6.23*	21	6.18	28	6.13	28
41.	There is a commitment to academic excellence on this campus.	6.20	25	6.22*	22	6.28	17	6.29	17
28.	Parking lots are well-lighted and secure.	6.13	32	6.21*	23	6.26	18	6.25	19
47.	Faculty provide timely feedback about student progress in a course.	6.18	27	6.21*	23	6.25	19	6.27	18

table continues

	First-Year (n=16,165)		Sophomore (n=7,789)		Junior (n=9,868)		Senior (n=10,639)	
Item	Score	Rank	Score	Rank	Score	Rank	Score	Rank
18. Library resources and services are adequate.	6.21	23	6.20*	25	6.25	19	6.25	19
72. On the whole, the campus is well-maintained.	6.23	19	6.19*	26	6.19	27	6.11	30
59. The institution shows concern for students as individuals.	6.18	27	6.19	26	6.20	26	6.20	24
49. There are adequate services to help me decide upon a career.	6.20	25	6.18*	28	6.13	32	6.10	33
4. Admissions staff are knowledgeable.	6.15	29	6.18	28	6.16	29	6.14	27
57. I seldom get the "run-around" when seeking information on this campus.	6.11	35	6.17*	30	6.24	24	6.25	19
27. The personnel involved in registration are helpful.	6.14	30	6.15	31	6.14	31	6.13	28
12. Financial aid awards are announced to students in time to be helpful in college planning.	6.12	34	6.14*	32	6.09	34	6.05	37
50. Class change (drop/add) policies are reasonable.	6.11	35	6.13	33	6.15	30	6.11	30
45. Students are made to feel welcome on this campus.	6.22	21	6.13*	33	6.09	34	6.03	40
11. Billing policies are reasonable.	6.00	41	6.10*	35	6.09	34	6.06	36
53. Faculty take into consideration student differences as they teach a course.	6.00	41	6.07*	36	6.06	39	6.05	37

table continues

	Item	First-Year (n=16,165)		Sophomore (n=7,789)		Junior (n=9,868)		Senior (n=10,639)	
		Score	Rank	Score	Rank	Score	Rank	Score	Rank
73.	Student activities fees are put to good use.	6.00	41	6.07*	36	6.05	42	6.03	40
35.	The assessment and course placement procedures are reasonable.	6.08	37	6.06	38	6.06	39	6.04	39
70.	Graduate teaching assistants are competent as classroom instructors.	6.14	30	6.06*	38	6.07	38	6.01	42
51.	This institution has a good reputation within the community.	6.06	39	6.06	38	6.10	33	6.09	34
3.	Faculty care about me as an individual.	5.99	45	6.05*	41	6.08	37	6.11	30
5.	Financial aid counselors are helpful.	5.96	49	6.02*	42	6.00	44	5.97	43
19.	My academic advisor helps me set goals to work toward.	5.98	47	6.01*	43	6.04	43	5.96	45
61.	Adjunct faculty are competent as classroom instructors.	6.00	41	6.01*	43	6.06	39	6.07	35
67.	Freedom of expression is protected on campus.	6.03	40	6.00*	45	5.95	46	5.92	47
32.	Tutoring services are readily available.	6.13	33	5.99*	46	5.86	52	5.73	57
44.	Academic support services adequately meet the needs of students.	5.99	45	5.95*	47	5.93	48	5.88	49
71.	Channels for expressing student complaints are readily available.	5.91	56	5.94	48	5.96	45	5.97	43

table continues

	Item	First-Year (n=16,165)		Sophomore (n=7,789)		Junior (n=9,868)		Senior (n=10,639)	
		Score	Rank	Score	Rank	Score	Rank	Score	Rank
15.	The staff in the health services area are competent.	5.96	49	5.94*	48	5.89	51	5.84	50
22.	Counseling staff care about students as individuals.	5.98	47	5.92*	50	5.91	50	5.82	51
20.	The business office is open during hours which are convenient for most students.	5.94	52	5.92	50	5.95	46	5.93	46
63.	Student disciplinary procedures are fair.	5.94	52	5.88*	52	5.81	54	5.78	53
62.	There is a strong commitment to racial harmony on this campus.	5.89	57	5.88*	52	5.86	52	5.82	51
23.	Living conditions in the residence halls are comfortable (adequate space, lighting, heat, air conditioning, telephones, etc.)	6.22	21	5.87*	54	5.58	63	5.42	66
43.	Admissions counselors respond to prospective students' unique needs and requests.	5.93	54	5.85*	55	5.81	54	5.77	54
13.	Library staff are helpful and approachable.	5.85	59	5.85*	55	5.92	49	5.92	47
64.	New student orientation services help students adjust to college.	5.95	51	5.81*	57	5.71	58	5.65	59
10.	Administrators are approachable to students.	5.81	63	5.81*	57	5.79	56	5.75	55
54.	Bookstore staff are helpful.	5.78	65	5.78	59	5.79	56	5.74	56

table continues

	Item	First-Year (*n*=16,165)		Sophomore (*n*=7,789)		Junior (*n*=9,868)		Senior (*n*=10,639)	
		Score	Rank	Score	Rank	Score	Rank	Score	Rank
48.	Admissions counselors accurately portray the campus in their recruiting practices.	5.84	60	5.77*	60	5.69	60	5.66	58
46.	I can get easily involved in campus organizations.	5.86	58	5.75*	61	5.59	62	5.52	61
60.	I generally know what's happening on campus.	5.82	62	5.72*	62	5.61	61	5.51	62
37.	I feel a sense of pride about my campus.	5.81	63	5.72*	62	5.70	59	5.64	60
38.	There is an adequate selection of food available in the cafeteria.	5.93	54	5.71*	64	5.58	63	5.48	64
1.	Most students feel a sense of belonging here.	5.73	66	5.62*	65	5.51	67	5.42	66
52.	The student center is a comfortable place for students to spend their leisure time.	5.65	69	5.60*	66	5.56	65	5.51	62
56.	The student handbook provides helpful information about campus life.	5.71	67	5.60*	66	5.53	66	5.47	65
40.	Residence hall regulations are reasonable.	5.84	60	5.54*	68	5.28	69	5.14	69
31.	Males and females have equal opportunities to participate in intercollegiate athletics.	5.57	71	5.44*	69	5.29	68	5.20	68
42.	There are a sufficient number of weekend activities for students.	5.62	70	5.36*	70	5.18	70	5.06	70

table continues

	Item	First-Year (n=16,165)		Sophomore (n=7,789)		Junior (n=9,868)		Senior (n=10,639)	
		Score	Rank	Score	Rank	Score	Rank	Score	Rank
30.	Residence hall staff are concerned about me as an individual.	5.66	68	5.35*	71	5.13	72	4.97	71
24.	The intercollegiate athletic programs contribute to a strong sense of school spirit.	5.46	72	5.26*	72	5.16	71	4.96	72
9.	A variety of intramural activities are offered.	5.13	73	4.96*	73	4.77	73	4.60	73

Note: * indicates that sophomores differ significantly from at least one other class level ($p < .05$).

Table 6

A Comparison of Public College Students across Class Level on Issues of Satisfaction (N=44,461)

	Item	First-Year (*n*=16,165)		Sophomore (*n*=7,789)		Junior (*n*=9,868)		Senior (*n*=10,639)	
		Score	Rank	Score	Rank	Score	Rank	Score	Rank
68.	Nearly all of the faculty are knowledgeable in their field.	5.64	2	5.49	1	5.44	1	5.39	1
72.	On the whole, the campus is well-maintained.	5.60	4	5.40	2	5.38	2	5.29	2
65.	Faculty are usually available after class and during office hours.	5.54	5	5.34	3	5.29	5	5.25	5
51.	This institution has a good reputation within the community.	5.61	3	5.33	4	5.25	6	5.13	11
39.	I am able to experience intellectual growth here.	5.48	8	5.31	5	5.34	3	5.28	3
69.	There is a good variety of courses provided on this campus.	5.73	1	5.30	6	5.21	9	5.08	12
8.	The content of courses within my major is valuable.	5.35	15	5.27	7	5.30	4	5.20	7
33.	My academic advisor is knowledgeable about requirements in my major.	5.50	7	5.27	7	5.25	6	5.26	4
7.	The campus is safe and secure for all students.	5.38	14	5.21	9	5.14	11	5.14	10
18.	Library resources and services are adequate.	5.43	10	5.19	10	5.06	15	4.91	18
13.	Library staff are helpful and approachable.	5.19	29	5.18	11	5.20	10	5.24	6
16.	The instruction in my major field is excellent.	5.20	28	5.17	12	5.25	6	5.19	8

table continues

	Item	First-Year (n=16,165)		Sophomore (n=7,789)		Junior (n=9,868)		Senior (n=10,639)	
		Score	Rank	Score	Rank	Score	Rank	Score	Rank
29.	It is an enjoyable experience to be a student on this campus.	5.44	9	5.16	13	5.06	15	4.94	16
54.	Bookstore staff are helpful.	5.33	17	5.14	14	5.09	12	4.98	14
6.	My academic advisor is approachable.	5.52	6	5.13	15	5.08	13	5.15	9
55.	Major requirements are clear and reasonable.	5.25	21	5.08	16	5.01	18	4.97	15
67.	Freedom of expression is protected on campus.	5.40	13	5.08	16	5.01	18	4.88	21
45.	Students are made to feel welcome on this campus.	5.43	10	5.08	16	4.97	20	4.89	20
58.	The quality of instruction I receive in most of my classes is excellent.	5.19	29	5.06	19	5.07	14	5.02	13
32.	Tutoring services are readily available.	5.42	12	5.04	20	4.79	32	4.72	34
41.	There is a commitment to academic excellence on this campus.	5.30	19	5.03	21	5.02	17	4.91	18
31.	Males and females have equal opportunities to participate in intercollegiate athletics.	5.26	20	5.03	21	4.88	24	4.82	24
50.	Class change (drop/add) policies are reasonable.	5.34	16	5.01	23	4.94	21	4.93	17
9.	A variety of intramural activities are offered.	5.22	24	5.00	24	4.88	25	4.80	26
26.	Computer labs are adequate and accessible.	5.17	32	4.99	25	4.84	29	4.72	34

table continues

Item		First-Year (n=16,165)		Sophomore (n=7,789)		Junior (n=9,868)		Senior (n=10,639)	
		Score	Rank	Score	Rank	Score	Rank	Score	Rank
46.	I can get easily involved in campus organizations.	5.23	22	4.96	26	4.86	26	4.87	22
1.	Most students feel a sense of belonging here.	5.15	36	4.94	27	4.82	30	4.73	33
66.	Tuition paid is a worthwhile investment.	5.20	27	4.94	27	4.91	22	4.84	23
56.	The student handbook provides helpful information about campus life.	5.23	22	4.94	27	4.85	27	4.76	28
37.	I feel a sense of pride about my campus.	5.32	18	4.94	27	4.89	23	4.74	32
52.	The student center is a comfortable place for students to spend their leisure time.	5.17	32	4.93	31	4.85	27	4.76	28
2.	The campus staff are caring and helpful.	5.22	24	4.91	32	4.82	30	4.75	31
62.	There is a strong commitment to racial harmony on this campus.	5.19	29	4.87	33	4.79	32	4.70	38
25.	Faculty are fair and unbiased in their treatment of individual students.	5.22	24	4.86	34	4.79	32	4.67	40
14.	My academic advisor is concerned about my success as an individual.	5.17	32	4.83	35	4.77	37	4.82	24
61.	Adjunct faculty are competent as classroom instructors.	5.03	44	4.83	35	4.78	35	4.79	27
63.	Student disciplinary procedures are fair.	5.12	37	4.82	37	4.78	35	4.72	34

table continues

129

	Item	First-Year (n=16,165)		Sophomore (n=7,789)		Junior (n=9,868)		Senior (n=10,639)	
		Score	Rank	Score	Rank	Score	Rank	Score	Rank
27.	The personnel involved in registration are helpful.	5.11	38	4.81	38	4.71	40	4.62	44
4.	Admissions staff are knowledgeable.	5.10	40	4.79	39	4.64	44	4.52	50
64.	New student orientation services help students adjust to college.	5.11	38	4.79	39	4.67	43	4.63	42
20.	The business office is open during hours which are convenient for most students.	4.95	47	4.78	41	4.73	39	4.66	41
35.	The assessment and course placement procedures are reasonable.	5.04	43	4.78	41	4.74	38	4.71	37
49.	There are adequate services to help me decide upon a career.	5.10	40	4.77	43	4.71	40	4.59	45
44.	Academic support services adequately meet the needs of students.	5.03	44	4.75	44	4.64	44	4.56	47
70.	Graduate teaching assistants are competent as classroom instructors.	5.06	42	4.74	45	4.59	48	4.57	46
15.	The staff in the health services area are competent.	4.88	53	4.69	46	4.60	46	4.63	42
48.	Admissions counselors accurately portray the campus in their recruiting practices.	5.01	46	4.69	46	4.57	50	4.51	51
10.	Administrators are approachable to students.	4.92	50	4.68	48	4.56	51	4.45	53

table continues

		First-Year (n=16,165)		Sophomore (n=7,789)		Junior (n=9,868)		Senior (n=10,639)	
	Item	Score	Rank	Score	Rank	Score	Rank	Score	Rank
47.	Faculty provide timely feedback about student progress in a course.	4.77	63	4.67	49	4.71	40	4.76	28
3.	Faculty care about me as an individual.	4.81	59	4.64	50	4.60	46	4.69	39
60.	I generally know what's happening on campus.	4.88	53	4.64	50	4.52	52	4.45	53
59.	The institution shows concern for students as individuals.	4.93	48	4.63	52	4.50	54	4.44	55
36.	Security staff respond quickly in emergencies.	4.93	48	4.63	52	4.59	48	4.55	48
43.	Admissions counselors respond to prospective students' unique needs and requests.	4.90	52	4.60	54	4.49	55	4.41	57
22.	Counseling staff care about students as individuals.	4.78	60	4.55	55	4.45	57	4.40	59
28.	Parking lots are well-lighted and secure.	4.82	58	4.55	55	4.51	53	4.48	52
24.	The intercollegiate athletic programs contribute to a strong sense of school spirit.	5.17	32	4.54	57	4.44	58	4.17	67
53.	Faculty take into consideration student differences as they teach a course.	4.78	60	4.52	58	4.47	56	4.42	56
19.	My academic advisor helps me set goals to work toward.	4.86	56	4.50	59	4.44	58	4.41	57
11.	Billing policies are reasonable.	4.72	65	4.49	60	4.43	60	4.37	60

table continues

Item	First-Year (n=16,165)		Sophomore (n=7,789)		Junior (n=9,868)		Senior (n=10,639)	
	Score	Rank	Score	Rank	Score	Rank	Score	Rank
40. Residence hall regulations are reasonable.	4.87	55	4.49	60	4.37	62	4.33	62
5. Financial aid counselors are helpful.	4.68	67	4.47	62	4.36	63	4.30	63
30. Residence hall staff are concerned about me as an individual.	4.91	51	4.44	63	4.28	65	4.21	66
34. I am able to register for classes I need with few conflicts.	4.84	57	4.40	64	4.42	61	4.54	49
71. Channels for expressing student complaints are readily available.	4.78	62	4.35	65	4.19	68	4.05	68
12. Financial aid awards are announced to students in time to be helpful in college planning.	4.71	66	4.34	66	4.26	66	4.22	64
17. Adequate financial aid is available for most students.	4.67	68	4.33	67	4.34	64	4.37	60
73. Student activities fees are put to good use.	4.77	63	4.23	68	4.06	71	3.88	71
42. There are a sufficient number of weekend activities for students.	4.62	69	4.13	69	4.07	70	3.92	70
38. There is an adequate selection of food available in the cafeteria.	4.25	72	4.09	70	4.22	67	4.22	64
57. I seldom get the "run-around" when seeking information on this campus.	4.57	70	4.09	70	3.91	72	3.73	72

table continues

Item	First-Year (n=16,165)		Sophomore (n=7,789)		Junior (n=9,868)		Senior (n=10,639)	
	Score	Rank	Score	Rank	Score	Rank	Score	Rank
23. Living conditions in the residence halls are comfortable (adequate space, lighting, heat, air conditioning, telephones, etc.)	4.44	71	4.08	72	4.08	69	4.05	68
21. The amount of student parking space on campus is adequate.	3.08	73	2.68	73	2.58	73	2.54	73

Note: * Sophomores differ significantly from at least one other class level on all items ($p < .05$).

The Sophomore Slump:
An Annotated Bibliography

by Stephanie M. Foote

B

Appendix

Currently, very little research exists specifically about the "sophomore year experience;" however, based on institutional retention rates, many colleges are recognizing that students are not only leaving after their first year of college, but after the second year as well. As many as 85% of those students who drop out of college will choose to do so during their first two years (Astin, 1975).

The purpose of this annotated bibliography is to present a selection of print and electronic resources focusing primarily on the sophomore slump. The resources have been grouped into three basic categories: (a) "College Transitions" provides basic insight into the critical transitions for college students; (b)"The Sophomore Slump Defined" focuses specifically on the sophomore transition; and (c) "Combating the Sophomore Slump" offers strategies to assist faculty and staff in combating the negative outcomes associated with the sophomore year transition.

The final section highlights sophomore programs from several institutions. The components and content of these programs vary, but all focus on meeting the needs of their sophomore populations.

to annotated bibliography ▶

College Transitions

Astin, A. W. (1977). *Four critical years: The effect of college on beliefs, attitudes, and knowledge.* San Francisco: Jossey-Bass.

Astin, A. W. (1993). What matters in college? Four critical years revisited. San Francisco: Jossey-Bass.

> *In Four Critical Years, Astin examines the data compiled from the Cooperative Institutional Research Program (CIRP) survey regarding the impact of college, student attitudes, and beliefs. The data support many of the concepts associated with the sophomore slump (i.e., poor class attendance, involvement in extra-curricular activities both academic and non-academic). He also offers suggestions for changing policy and procedures based on the outcomes of the research. What Matters in College? revisits the issues addressed in Four Critical Years with new findings from the CIRP survey. Like its predecessor, this book supports concepts associated with the sophomore slump.*

Banning, J. H. (1989). Impact of college environments on freshman students. In M. L. Upcraft, J. N. Gardner, & Associates (Eds.), *The freshman year experience* (p. 53-62). San Francisco: Jossey-Bass.

> *The author examines the effects of the college environment on first-year students and provides various theories to support the first year as a transitional period when the ecology of college (i.e., environment and/or stimuli in the form of new people and living arrangements, peer pressure, etc.) has a profound impact on new students. The author also suggests environmental strategies for intervening during the first year. Many of the suggested strategies can be expanded to assist sophomores as well.*

Juillerat, S. (1995). *Investigating a two-dimensional approach to the assessment of student satisfaction: Validation of the student satisfaction inventory.* Unpublished doctoral dissertation, Temple University.

> *The author examines the history of student satisfaction assessments, beginning with an instrument used in the 1960's, to the results from a sample of students who took the Student Satisfaction Inventory. Student retention and the justification for institutional retention efforts are explored in this dissertation, including various theories supporting different methods of assessment. Much of the history, theoretical perspectives, and satisfaction inventories can be utilized to understand the sophomore transition, as well as to assist in refining services for students.*

Pascarella, E., & Terenzini, P. (1991). *How college affects students: Findings and insights from twenty years of research.* San Francisco: Jossey-Bass.

> *This book explores the effects of college on students, touching on the development of cognitive skills and intellectual growth; moral values, attitudes, and beliefs; developmental theory and personal changes (i.e., identity, self-esteem, etc.); career decision; benefits of attending college, including quality of life and economic benefits. The authors compile twenty years of research in higher education to explain the various transitions which college students experience.*

Schreiner, L. (1996, July). *Who stays, who leaves, and why?* Paper presented at the National Conference on Student Retention, Orlando, FL.

> *The paper outlines several myths of retention and explains the reality of these myths. Further, the author provides an overview of retention theory and research and examines the impact of institutional intervention or failure to intervene. The author also includes profiles of both the "at-risk" and the persistent student, along with some predictors of first-year GPA. While this information is useful in predicting the success or failure of first-year students, it can also be used to develop strategies to retain all students. Moreover, retention data may help educators better understand the nature of the transition to college and better predict which students will make this transition successfully.*

Tinto, V. (1993). *Leaving college: Rethinking the causes and cures of student attrition.* Chicago: The University of Chicago Press.

> *The author explores student departure (including who tends to leave higher education, and why), and what action institutions can take to combat student attrition (i.e., renewing the institution's educational, social, and intellectual commitment, identifying at-risk students, monitoring student progress, and establishing early intervention programs). Although the book focuses primarily on the retention of first-year students, the key retention concepts can also be applied to sophomores.*

The Sophomore Slump Defined

Lemons, L. J., & Douglas, R. (1987). A developmental perspective on the sophomore slump. *NASPA Journal, 24*(3), 15-19.

> *This article provides a definition of the sophomore slump based on the findings of several academicians. The authors draw on four of Arthur Chickering's seven vectors of student development to explain what sophomores experience during their period of transition. A section is devoted to intervention strategies that student affairs professionals can employ, and the authors highlight several sophomore programs.*

Coburn, K. L., & Treeger, M. L. (1997). *Letting go: A parent's guide to understanding the college years* (3rd edition). New York: Harper Perennial.

> *In addition to providing information about what to expect during orientation and the first year of college, the authors devote a chapter to the "Sophomore Year and Beyond." This chapter offers some of the characteristics and needs of sophomore students and includes personal accounts from former sophomores about their experiences during this transitional year. Other sections focus on choosing a major, stopping out, moving off-campus, transferring, studying abroad, and making commitments on campus.*

Combating the Sophomore Slump

Backhus, D. (1989). Centralized intrusive advising and undergraduate retention. *NACADA Journal, 9*(1), 39-45.

> *Dewayne Backhus describes the Student Advising Center (SAC) at Emporia State University (ESU). The SAC was established by ESU to advise all first-year and undeclared students. Advisement is conducted from a developmental perspective. A study that compared a pre-SAC student cohort to SAC participants revealed that students who were advised by the SAC had a rate of retention 8% higher than those who were not. The author asserts that the services of the Student Advising Center are responsible for this positive difference, since no discernible treatment variable exists other than the presence of the centralized student advising service.*

Carter, C. (1990). *Majoring In the Rest of Your Life*. New York: The Noonday Press.

> *Carol Carter has written a text that helps students choose a career and gives them specific suggestions they can use from their first year of college and on. The book is divided into thirteen chapters that address the following career/future-related topics: planning/organization, problem solving/analytical skills, creativity/innovativeness, drive/energy, teamwork, people management, leadership, common-sense smarts, independence/tenacity, personal adaptability, communication, marketing oneself, interpersonal skills, stress tolerance, and results/goal orientation. The book also includes five appendices: companies with summer/winter internships, books for further reference, associations and organizations for college students (alternative education, honor societies, professional fraternities, membership organizations, pre-professional organizations, social welfare, volunteer organizations), graduate school application, and educational opportunities following graduation. Related topic heading(s): Freshman Seminar Resources.*

Erkut, S., & Mokros, J. R. (1984). Professors as models and mentors for college students. *American Educational Research Journal, 21*(2), 399-417.

> *Sophomores and seniors in five coeducational and one women's liberal arts college were surveyed to provide some insight into the gender-related patterns in the modeling-mentoring relationships between college students and their professors. Findings showed that female students neither gravitated toward nor avoided female role models, while men, on the other hand, avoided female role models. Women, especially those choosing female role models, looked for mentors who could provide information on how to combine family and professional aspirations. Male and female responses showed more similarities than differences. Gender differences in the impact of a mentor for women related to the type of college the women attended. Women at single sex colleges with male mentors were found to be more successful academically, felt more successful relative to their peers – both male and female – and planned to attend graduate or professional school at rates higher than any other group.*

Fidler, P. P. (1991). Relationship of freshman orientation seminars to sophomore return rates. *Journal of the Freshman Year Experience, 3*(1), 7-38.

> *This article explores 16 years of data compiled regarding the sophomore return rate for students who participated in University 101 (the first-year seminar) at the University of South Carolina in comparison to students who did not participate. The author suggests sophomore retention rates are improved through participation in University 101.*

Juillerat, S. (2000, February). *The neglected sophomore.* Paper presented at the Nineteenth Annual Conference on The First-Year Experience, Columbia, SC.

> *The results of over 100,000 students who took the Student Satisfaction Inventory are outlined in this paper. The author gathered responses from sophomores attending both private and public institutions and compared their overall satisfaction on issues related to student services, faculty availability, the quality of education, and the institution itself. Taking their responses into consideration, the author makes some suggestions regarding the needs of these students.*

Noel, L., & Levitz, R. (1991, November). Beating the sophomore slump. *Recruitment and Retention in Higher Education, 5*(11), 1-3.

> *This article highlights the efforts of Beloit College to assist sophomore students during their transition from lower- to upper-classmen. The authors outline the research, placing emphasis on the development of an instrument used to gage the retention rate among sophomores at selected Midwest colleges, and the subsequent retention efforts Beloit College has employed for sophomore students.*

Schreiner, L. (2000, February). *Advising strategies for sophomore success.* Paper presented at the Nineteenth Annual Conference on The First-Year Experience, Columbia, SC.

> *This paper offers a definition of the "sophomore slump" (including several definitions from students who participated in a focus group), what services/aspects of college that sophomores find significant (based on the Student Satisfaction Inventory), advising issues for sophomores, and strategies to help combat these issues.*

Schwebel, S., (1995. September 16). Advising aims to prevent dreaded sophomore slump. *Yale Daily News.* Retrieved from the World Wide Web: http://www.yale.edu/ydn/paper/9.16/9.16.95storyno.CC.html

> *The quality and availability of sophomore advising at Yale are the issues addressed in this article. In addition to several quotes from students regarding the quality of advising, the article provides information about Yale's one-evening residential advising program.*

Tomb, L. S (Winter, 1999). The sophomore slump or how to choose a major. *Parent Line* Retrieved from the World Wide Web: www.alumni.wesleyan.edu/WWW/Info/Parents/p111p1.html

> *This article, targeted at parents of sophomore students, concentrates on the major and career counseling Wesleyan employs to retain sophomore students. It also offers the rationale behind the focus of the institution's retention efforts.*

Wilder, J. S. (1993). The sophomore slump: A complex developmental period that contributes to attrition. *College Student Affairs Journal, 12*(2), 18-27.

> *The article highlights research conducted on students who were classified as "decliners," or those who earned a 2.75-4.0 GPA their first year and subsequently declined from there. In addition to those whose GPA declined, students who either maintained or increased their GPA ("maintainers") during two semesters were also subjects of the research. While "decliners" were more likely to be involved in non-academic activities than maintainers, they also experienced a lower sense of school spirit, had little contact with academic advisors, and tended to be absent from classes more often than their counterparts. The author makes some suggestions for overcoming "the sophomore slump" which include heightened interaction among students, staff, and faculty and specific programming for sophomores.*

Wilson, R. C., & Woods, L. (1974). Social-psychological accessibility and faculty-student interaction beyond the classroom. *Sociology of Education, 47*(1), 74-92.

Faculty members at six different colleges and universities were surveyed for this study. Their responses indicate that the amount of faculty interaction with students outside the classroom is directly related to their accessibility for such interaction. The most important indicators of this accessibility were the teaching practices used in class. These practices included inviting students to help make class plans or policy via course evaluations or discussions, discussing points of view other than those of the instructor, giving essay rather than objective exams and not grading on a curve. Data suggesting some of the consequences of out-of-class interaction with students for faculty also are presented. These consequences include increased job satisfaction and better knowledge about students' academic strengths and weaknesses.

Specific Programs Targeted at Sophomores

• St. Michael's College (Vermont) has an Office of Sophomore Programs and Development. Additionally, the college offers sophomore housing and programs centered around career development, and beating the "sophomore slump."

• Beloit College (Wisconsin) has a "Sophomore Year Program," which includes a sophomore retreat, an Exploration and Declaration Major Fair, and a comprehensive academic plan (helping sophomores plan their remaining years at Beloit).

• Spartanburg Methodist College (Spartanburg, South Carolina) offers SMC 103, a continuation of SMC 101 and SMC 102 (first-year seminar courses). SMC 103 is designed to enhance the traditional liberal arts education and emphasizes attendance at cultural events.

• University of Indianapolis (Indianapolis, Indiana) requires sophomores to take a Lecture/Performance Series to compliment their liberal arts education.

Edward "Chip" Anderson has been an administrator and member of UCLA's teaching faculty for more than 30 years. In addition, he is now a professor in Azusa Pacific University's doctoral program in Educational Leadership and Master's Program in College Student Affairs. He has published on college student retention, academic achievement, and strengths-based approaches to academic and personal success. He has consulted and conducted training programs at nearly 100 colleges and universities.

Bayard (By) Baylis serves as Vice President for Academic Affairs and Dean of the University at Indiana Wesleyan University. He began his teaching career at The King's College (NY) where for 15 years he served in various faculty and administrative positions. He also served for 11 years in a number of administrative positions at Messiah College (PA). His doctoral studies in mathematics at the University of Delaware focused on the interface of topology and analysis. He has co-authored three statistics textbooks and is a frequent presenter at national and international assessment conferences. He served as the main author of two FIPSE grants for the Council for Christian Colleges & Universities (CCCU) and was co-director of its Collaborative Assessment Project: Taking Values Seriously: Assessing the Mission of Church-Related Higher Education.

Michael Boivin is presently Professor of Psychology at Indiana Wesleyan University in Marion, Indiana, where he has served since 1996. He also has an adjunct research appointment with the Neuropsychology Program in the Department of Psychiatry at the University of Michigan. His principal research interest is the effect of chronic infectious diseases on the neuropsychological development of children in the tropics, and he has published dozens of articles and presentation abstracts stemming from work as a Fulbright scholar in the Congo, Africa, as well as in Laos and Senegal. Throughout his 22 years of teaching in the Christian liberal-arts college setting, he has also been instrumental in developing innovative intercultural and service-learning initiatives linked to assessment of outcomes and student portfolio building for psychology majors. More recently, he co-authored several successful grant initiatives involving students in interdisciplinary scholarship and mentoring in order to enhance student success and retention at Indiana Wesleyan University.

About the authors

Michael Boston is the former Assistant Manager of Tarkington Hall at Purdue University.

Roxanne S. DuVivier is the Vice President of Student Affairs at Hocking College (Ohio) and holds an adjunct professorship in the School of Applied Behavioral Sciences at Ohio University. She is a licensed counseling psychologist and noted authority on learning and cognition. She has led numerous national and international workshops on learning profiling, instructional design, and the development of learner-centered communities. In addition to this work, she is a program consultant and trainer for the Noel Levitz USA Group specializing in student retention, academic advising, and learning enhancement systems. DuVivier has written numerous articles and authored a text entitled *Diagnosis and Treatment in Education* (University Press of America, 1992). She received her Ph.D. from Ohio University.

Scott E. Evenbeck earned a B.A. in psychology from Indiana University and an M.A. and Ph.D. in social psychology from the University of North Carolina at Chapel Hill. Currently, he is an Associate Professor of Psychology at Indiana University Purdue University Indianapolis (IUPUI). He has served in several administrative positions including Associate Dean of the Faculties and Director of Continuing Studies at IUPUI. He has also served as a member of an instructional team for a learning community course geared toward first-year students. Evenbeck is currently Dean of the University College.

Stephanie M. Foote is Coordinator of the Academic Peer Advisor Internship Program and an Academic Advisor in the Academic Advising Center at the State University of New York at Stony Brook. She received her B.A. from Coastal Carolina University and her M.Ed. from the University of South Carolina where she worked with University 101 and The National Resource Center for The First-Year Experience and Students in Transition. Foote is an active member of NACADA and ACPA; she has also presented and published about the transition from high school to college, the first-year experience, and

the use of peer leaders in the first-year seminar classroom.

Gwen A. Fountain is currently Interim President of Butler University in Indianapolis, Indiana. She was previously Dean of Academic Affairs at Butler University. Her Ph.D. and M.A. are in economics from the University of Michigan. Fountain's areas of interest are in student development, learning styles, and teaching/learning strategies.

Jerry G. Gaff is Vice President of the Association of American Colleges and Universities. He has directed national projects to strengthen undergraduate general education programs and to develop new models for the graduate preparation of future faculty members. He also is the founding director of the Network for Academic Renewal that assists administrators and faculty members in improving their academic programs in such ways as internationalizing the curriculum, using diversity and technology to aid learning, and developing more quality and coherence in the general education curricula. He has published three books on curriculum issues: *General Education Today* (1983), *New Life for the College Curriculum* (1991), and *Strong Foundations: Twelve Principles of Effective General Education Programs* (1994). He has also assisted scores of institutions to strengthen their core curricula.

John N. Gardner is Senior Fellow of the National Resource Center for The First-Year Experience and Students in Transition and Distinguished Professor Emeritus of Library and Information Science at the University of South Carolina. Gardner administered the University 101 program at the University of South Carolina for 23 years and founded the National Resource Center in 1986, serving as its Executive Director until 1999. Gardner currently serves as Executive Director of the Policy Center on the First Year of College, funded by a grant from The Pew Charitable Trusts, and based at Brevard College, Brevard, N.C. He is also appointed there as Distinguished Professor of Educational Leadership. The Policy Center works with colleges and universities around the nation to develop and share a range of first-year assessment procedures and tools. In turn, these will be used to measure the effectiveness of existing institutional programs, policies and structures that affect first-year students.

Philip D. Gardner is Director of the Collegiate Employment Research Institute at Michigan State University where he and his staff study issues related to the transition from college to the workplace. In addition, his responsibilities extend to coordinating assessment programs for the University's colleges and departments. Recently he was asked to design a course for sophomores that emphasizes the connections between interests and academics with the objective of engaging sophomores in academic and co-curricular experiences. He has published widely on issues related to cooperative work, skill development, early socialization in the workplace, and gender differences in technology usage and salaries. Gardner received his undergraduate degree in chemistry from Whitman College and his M.S. and Ph.D. in resource economics and public policy at Michigan State University. He worked in Thailand on agricultural land reform and served on the faculty at the University of California, Riverside before returning to MSU in his current position.

Kaylene Hallberg is the Dean of Student Services and Special Projects for the California Community College Chancellor's Office, located in Sacramento California. The Chancellor's Office serves 108 community colleges and 72 districts in the state of California. Hallberg holds degrees from San Francisco State University and Azusa Pacific College.

Stephanie Juillerat is an Associate Professor of Psychology at Azusa Pacific University in Azusa, California. She received her Ph.D. from Temple University in group and organizational psychology with an emphasis in psychometrics. Her research focuses on the link between student satisfaction and retention, and she is the co-author of *The Student Satisfaction Inventory*, a nationally published measure of student satisfaction. Juillerat presents her satisfaction research

at numerous conferences and also serves as an educational consultant to colleges and universities through her work as a lead researcher on the Comprehensive Assessment Project, which is conducted by the Council for Christian Colleges and Universities. She is an active member of the American Psychological Association, the American Psychological Society, and the American Association for Higher Education.

Jerry Pattengale is a frequent presenter at universities and conferences, and has helped to develop numerous award-winning programs, such as the *Virtual Advising Link Program* (NACADA, 1999), the *Odyssey In Egypt* virtual curriculum (NII international web award, 1996), and the strategic retention plan at Indiana Wesleyan University (various awards, 1996-2000), where he serves as the Associate Dean for Academic Affairs. He also helped to found the "Night of Champions" in Los Angeles (serving 5,000 students annually), *The Scriptorium* (Grand Haven, MI, and Hampton Court, Herefordshire, England) and *Heads Up Baseball* (headsupbaseball.org). In 2000, Houghton Mifflin Publishing and the University of South Carolina's National Resource Center presented him with the national "Outstanding First-Year Advocate" award. Azusa Pacific students voted him "Professor of the Year" (1993, 1995), and he received the "Alpha Chi Honors Society Teacher of the Year Award" (1994). He has contributed to a variety of publications, including author of *Heads Up Choices*, co-author of *Consider the Source*, and chapters in *Historical Dictionary of the Modern Olympic Movement*, *On Your Mark*, *Events That Changed America in the Twentieth Century*, *The Anchor Bible Dictionary* (6 vols.), *Great Events from History: Human Rights*, and the forthcoming *Dictionary of Biblical Manners and Customs*. He is currently working on *The Dream Needs To Be Stronger Than the Struggle*, a book on intrinsic motivation.

Laurie A. Schreiner is currently Professor of Psychology and Associate Academic Dean at Eastern College, a private liberal arts college in the suburbs of Philadelphia. She received her Ph.D. in Community Psychology from the University of Tennessee in 1982 and has taught in private liberal arts colleges since that time. She has chaired retention committees, academic councils, and curriculum committees, has coordinated first-year advising programs and first-year student seminars, and has consulted with more than 100 colleges and universities nationally on issues of retention, student satisfaction, advising, and first-year programs. She is co-author of *The Student Satisfaction Inventory* and has authored validity studies of the *College Student Inventory* and *Career Quest*. She is currently Project Director of two separate grants awarded by the Fund for the Improvement of Post--Secondary Education, one for dissemination of a successful first-year program, and one for a strengths-based campus-wide approach to student retention, with a particular focus on the sophomore year.